AFRICAN JOURNAL
by
Leslie J. Price

Leslie Jones Price was born in Kentucky and now resides in Greenville, South Carolina. She received her B.A. from the University of Kentucky and her M.S.J. degree from the Medill School of Journalism, North-western University. She has been Director of Publicity at Mary Hardin Baylor College, a staff reporter for the Louisville *Courier-Journal* and for the *New Haven Register*, and a feature writer for other newspapers. Mrs. Price is married to Theron D. Price, emeritus professor of religion at Furman University. They have three children, Douglas, Sara Leslie, Philip, and five grandchildren.

"Autumn" from *The Selected Poems of Rainer Maria Rilke*, edited by Robert Bly. Copyright © 1981 by Robert Bly. Reprinted by permission of Harper & Row, Publishers, Inc.

New Hope
Birmingham, Alabama
© New Hope 1989
All Rights Reserved

Title: African Journal, by Leslie J. Price

Dewey Decimal Classification: 266.092

Subject Headings:

   Missions - Nigeria
   Missions, Foreign
   Missions, Volunteer
   Price, Leslie J.
   Price, Theron D.

Library of Congress 89-062250

ISBN 0-936625-73-2

N904101 • 7500 • 1089

Introduction

It was in Africa—in Nigeria—that I began for the first time daily and thoughtfully to listen to my inner voice, the one true voice that seemingly had escaped me through many years of seeking. There for nearly five months I was away from telephone, television, newspapers, committee meetings, entertaining, shopping malls, supermarkets, and a thousand goings and comings that make up the frenzied activity of life in the United States.

In West Africa I was immersed in a healing silence and a quietness of early morning solitude by the window and in the darkness of night where nothing shines but the moon and the stars. The brittle brown leaves falling from giant teak trees and the eerie clanging noise of the fruit bat announcing dawn were the only sounds to awaken me in those beginnings of magical days.

We went to Nigeria at the invitation of the Southern Baptist Foreign Mission Board. Price (which is what I call my husband) was to be guest professor at the Nigerian Baptist Theological Seminary in Ogbomosho, Nigeria. At that time a professor of religion at Furman University in Greenville, South Carolina, he was granted a semester leave of absence. After arriving at the seminary, I was asked to teach English to students' wives and journalism to men students.

Price was enthusiastic about going to teach in Nigeria. I was not as certain I should go. Here I was, a twentieth century, well-educated, well-traveled woman, yet my ignorance about Africa was appalling. I thought of snakes, tarantulas, malaria, mosquitoes, flies, and primitive living conditions. I thought of being so far removed from our three children, Douglas and Sara Leslie, both married with homes and children of their own, and Philip, our youngest, working

1

to finish college and achieve his own identity. I wondered if I might be going to the "jumping off place," a term my paternal grandmother used in the late 1920s, referring to any place far away.

At the same time I longed to share the excitement of travel with Price and the work that would be ours in Ogbomosho. I was attempting to get my spiritual house in order. I yearned—oh how I yearned—for some great reawakening of faith, to be blessed with a mystical experience, an epiphany. Somewhere, I reasoned, there must be a community of people among whom one could live, who practiced with their lives what they confessed as their faith. I was not looking for Utopia or saints, only a fellowship of believers who would inspire me, a pilgrim.

The more I dwelled on these thoughts, the more my mind and heart consented and turned toward going to Nigeria. On January 6th, 1978 Price and I left New York for five months in Ogbomosho.

I have always kept daily journals in our years of travel. This book is based on the writing in my daily Nigerian journal. These entries remind me of this unforgettable place and time in my life—a place where I feared going but toward which in a strange, unexplainable way I was being drawn. Once home, reading what I experienced there brought me to know that this God who watches over our lives was pulling me toward a deepening of my spiritual life. For there in Nigeria I lived with my consciousness attuned to the physical world around me and to my interior world. Many of these journal thoughts, I find, are concerned with what Thomas Merton called "a spiritual climate, an atmosphere, a landscape of the mind, a level of consciousness: the peace, the silence of aloneness, in which the Hearer listens."

My journey, outward and inward, was a part of times and conditions of the place that was Ogbomosho and Nigeria eleven years ago. Many changes in missionary personnel and in Nigeria have occurred since our departure.

I had made many other journeys before I came to West Africa—to Europe, South America, the Near East, the Middle East, and the Far East—but to this place I made the longest journey. That is the journey inward, closer to God. And as Rilke said "the inner journey is all that matters."

I dedicate *African Journal* in loving memory of my mother, Lillian Hart Jones.

JANUARY

Thursday, January 5th

Late evening and Price and I are in the departure lounge at Kennedy Airport, New York, getting ready to board a TWA 747 jet for Dakar in Senegal. The day has been a long one—earlier telling our youngest son, Philip, good-bye at the airport in Greenville, South Carolina, our home, then flying to LaGuardia Airport in New York, and finally from there by helicopter to Kennedy.

Now excitement recharges our batteries. We have an argument with an airline agent when we enter the TWA departure lounge. He insists that we cannot take aboard an extra piece of luggage even though it will fit under the plane seat. Price wins. He is 6 feet 6 inches tall and weighs close to 250 pounds, which can be intimidating, but even more convincing is his firm, deliberate, calm way of speaking. You know he means what he says and won't stand for anything that doesn't make sense. The agent relents and allows us to proceed into the lounge.

I notice the group around us. Men dressed in Western clothes who could be Africans or Americans. A young white couple looking serious and nervous. Several women with children but no one in African dress.

We board the sleek plane and fly into the night, soaring far above bright lights and dark ocean water. We speed at a pace hard to believe. We are fed, we see a movie, reading lights are turned on, then finally turned off. I am wide awake. Price sleeps with his head resting uncomfortably on the back of the seat that never fits his height. We have asked for and been assigned seats by the emergency door, where there is the greatest amount of room for long legs. It is also by toilets and most of the night some person is going or coming from there.

As much as I have flown, I am never ready for the feeling of flying in the dark. There is a sense of no world out there beyond the plane, and I am enclosed in a room from which I cannot escape, moving through dimensions of time and space I do not understand.

This night I push up the curtain at the window and see stars glittering far away and that is all. I settle deep into my seat and deeper into myself. We have a long journey before we will be home again and I, perhaps, an interior journey to make.

Excited yes, but apprehensive more. What is ahead for us? This in itself is stimulating, not to know what each day will bring, breaking out of a daily, fixed routine, seeing new sights, and meeting unknown people. For me the unknown challenges but at the same time can be fearful. Price never has any of these fears. His faith seems to me like a rock—solid, unbreakable, always strong. Mine has its ups and downs like a pebble tossed onto the sunlight of the beach and later swept into the murky ocean depths.

Late, toward 2:00 A.M. our time, I sleep. When we arrive in Senegal, it will be before daylight in another time zone.

Friday, January 6th

The plane touches ground at 6:40 A.M. on this January day at Yoff Airfield in Dakar, Senegal. Senegal is situated at the extreme of the West African continent bounded by Mauritania to the north and northeast, Mali to the east, and Guinea and Guinea-Bissau to the south. To the west is the Atlantic Ocean. Dakar is the capital city, located on the outermost tip or projection into the Atlantic known as Cape Verde. Many Senegalese speak French. In 1956, on the eve of African independence, France granted Senegal internal self-government. In 1959 the country gained political independence from France.

I slept little during the long night flight. Sleepy-eyed but excited, I gather up our bags while Price pulls out more luggage from sections overhead. We have a foot locker, filled with most of our clothes and a few books, to claim from the baggage area. From the plane, Price and I walk through the early morning darkness toward a small airport terminal. I sense a warming tropical heat and smell an earthy scent, mingling with a sea breeze and a pungent fragrance of flowers.

Farrell Runyan, middle-aged, graying, and pleasant-faced, greets us. He is with the Baptist mission in Dakar. I express regret that he has had to come at daybreak to meet us. He looks sleepy and tired, yet his welcome is a hearty one.

Slate gray light eases into the sky as we drive with him towards his house, not far from the Atlantic Ocean, sitting on flat, desert-dry land. Libby, his wife, a bustling, organized woman, has a breakfast waiting for us of sliced oranges, bacon, toast, jam and strong, hot coffee. We talk mainly by having our questions answered, but jet lag starts taking over. My ears buzz; my eyes feel weighted with coins. Price is sagging lower in his chair.

The Runyans sense that we need sleep and show us to our upstairs bedroom lighted by bright sunlight outside. Surprisingly, a strong wind gusts through the open windows. Libby says it is a wind from the Sahara called the *harmattan* that blows this time of the year. She tells me the large weird tree to the left of the house is a baobab tree and these are found everywhere in Africa. The Africans say it was condemned by God and stuck in the ground with its roots at the top. This giant tree is fascinating, with its eruption of branches in every direction from which hang long green balls on vine-like threads, resembling ornaments on a Christmas tree.

Suddenly I am wide awake, gazing out the window at scarlet and pink blooming hibiscus hedges, bright as a Matisse painting next to rock walls covered in purple blooming bougainvillea. Farther out the inky blue ocean shines, reflecting an identical colored sky. Two large hawks glide and dive overhead.

Yes, I muse, I think I am going to like living in Africa. These sights and vibrant colors assail my senses, making them come alive. Nature flourishes in abundance and rather pushes itself onto one's awareness.

Finally I lie down on the bed and sleep, in spite of the wild wind humming loudly around the corner wall. The near-fury of the wind delights me somehow. Price has gone fast asleep on the bed where he stretched out while I window-gazed. Would that I had his ability to sleep anywhere and everywhere no matter what the circumstances. He jokes and tells me it is because he has a clear conscience.

Saturday, January 7th

Today we are going with the Runyans on a small Senegalese ferry from Dakar out some miles in the ocean to Goree Island, once

Portuguese, then French occupied. The ferry is crowded with Senegalese women wearing long colorful dresses called boubous in shades of red, green, purple, or orange, and printed in designs of flowers, birds, or shells. The men wear similar shades and patterns of cloth made into trousers and long tunics. Most of these people laugh and talk noisily while we take our seats on the ferry.

Once on the rock-bordered island, we walk to see the slave house where some 300 Africans at a time were crowded into dungeon-like rooms underneath the first floor. From here, during the height of the slave trade to America, thousands were shipped in the dark holds of ships, chained throughout the voyage. The Senegalese were early participants in the slave trade, but most slaves were brought here from the Sudanic interior. Children were judged fit to send by the quality of their teeth, women by the look of their breasts. Husbands, wives, and children were separated, some taken, some left behind. Chained together, those departing walked down a narrow low passageway leading to a boat by the edge of the water.

I can almost hear their pitiful cries while we stand in this awful, silent place, knowing no adequate words to say. In a depressed mood, we return by ferry to Dakar.

Sunday, January 8th

Weary from jet lag and the high-pitched emotion of arriving and meeting new people, I slept soundly last night. Not once did I wake or dream. This morning the noisy wind that lulled me to sleep blows in a quieter mood. The weather is balmy, sunny and dry.

After breakfast, we go to a small, whitewashed Baptist church building. Price preaches in English and Runyan translates into French for the Senegalese congregation of perhaps 120 people. We remain in the building after the worship service for the wedding ceremony of a Senegalese young man, a student at the University of California, and his bride, a Portuguese young woman from Cape Verde. She wears a white satin, long wedding dress with train and carries flowers made of white satin. The groom wears an ivory-colored suit and navy shirt with white tie. Both bride and groom are good looking, their dark skins contrasting vividly against the white attire. She is going with him to California to live. This young woman will be like a fragile flower transplanted from a tropical garden to grow in a crowded flower bed along a busy, polluted highway.

Tonight we repack for our flight tomorrow toward Nigeria. On the way we will make brief stops at Bamako in Mali, Abidjan in the Ivory Coast, and Lome in Togo. To think that until this month I hardly knew these places existed! I like the sound of these mysterious, rhythmical names rolling off my tongue.

For it is now that our journey is to begin in the greatest and deepest sense, a far journey to relate to people not of our culture but even farther to travel distances within ourselves before we come home again.

Monday, January 9th

In the eerie light of dawn, we leave for the Dakar airport with Runyan driving. Poor man. Again he has to chauffeur us at an early hour. We want to call a taxi, but he insists on driving us there. We board an Air Afrique plane and soar over the ocean. More than three-fourths of the passengers on this plane are foreign people, with only a few Africans dressed in African style.

Nearing Bamako in Mali, I look down from the plane window and see green jungle below and, in a clearing of land, thatched-roof round huts clustered together. We get our first glimpse of the Niger River, still narrow here in the upper reaches. The river lies sleeping under the bright sunlight like a long, brown snake. I have a queer feeling that I'm seeing a movie passing before my eyes. Then a smiling stewardess serves us breakfast of papaya and pineapple slices, warm omelet, toast, jam, and coffee. We are in the twentieth century world up here thousands of feet high in the sky. I wonder what the people in those huts below are eating.

We stop briefly at Bamako. We walk quickly from the plane into the terminal, exercising our legs.

At Abidjan we deplane for lunch in the dining room of the airport where it is crowded, noisy and hot—no air conditioning. Surprisingly, we are served fresh cucumbers, tomatoes, carrots in a salad with a boiled egg on top and a rice dish mixed with strange-looking, dried-up pieces of meat. I push the meat and rice around on the plate with my fork and after one bite decide against eating any. Price eats his and has no bad aftereffects. Later from Togo, we fly on toward Lagos, the capital of Nigeria and land there in mid-afternoon.

I step off the plane and heat like the inside of a broiler oven assaults my skin and eyes. My legs feel as wobbly as sticks of straw from hours of sitting, but I want to turn and run from this heat to refuge in the plane. What is happening to me? I have traveled to many other countries before, even to India, the hottest weather experience. Waves of heat rise to my cheeks and a cold heaviness sits in my stomach. I am feeling claustrophobic as I often do in the midst of a large crowd. I want to yell, "I can't cope with this fear I'm feeling." But who would hear me in this mass of surging, loud-talking people heading for the passport control booths?

Instead I call frantically to Price, "Don't lose me," as we plunge through the crowd toward the passport official behind the nearest window. Men wearing long white tunics and trousers are everywhere. People yell at each other and bodies crush against bodies. A Japanese man in front of me has out his tape recorder. At last a stern-faced Nigerian officer lines up some of us in a single file, but people continue to push and press against us.

I scowl at Price. With his "what can we do about this" look he glances back at me. "Can't we get out of this mob?" I yell. "No, Leslie, you know we have to stay in line," he yells back. He is a calm, patient man, usually. His calmness makes me more agitated today. I want us to physically push against these bodies, move them out of the way, and get out of this confusion and heat.

Through the years I've managed to cope one way or another. What if I sat down on the floor here and wailed, "I want to go home." But I don't. I summon courage from a long ago part of me. Maybe it was born there when, at seventeen, a freshman at the University of Kentucky, I was homesick, teary-eyed, and wanting to return home. My parents drove a long way to see me. My Dad sat and talked to me that sultry autumn afternoon and among his words of wisdom were these firm ones: "You must learn to stand on your own feet and face life."

Finally we get through passport control, find our luggage, including our large footlocker, and trudge into the waiting room. No air conditioning—sweat runs down my face.

Thomas High, a teacher at the seminary in Ogbomosho, comes to greet us. He is a former student of Price's and is there to take us in his Land Rover "up country," as he says, where we are going to work and live for the next five months.

High and Price sit in the front seat where Price can accommodate his legs, and I ride in back along with a can of petrol. High says on long trips it is necessary to have car fuel of your own due to so few petrol stations.

10

The noise of the jeep and traffic on the road drowns out the conversation in front. I am too tired to talk anyway. I lean back against the seat and fan with a newspaper—no air conditioning anywhere, I realize. I have time to look and look seeing the people and the land, and to think my own thoughts.

Why had I agreed to go with Price to Africa in the first place? I had thought a long time about the hot climate, the threat of malaria, the primitive conditions, the deadly snakes, and being so far from our three children.

Yet I knew this would be an opportunity to help people. Maybe we did have something to share, I began to believe. I thought about how good it would be to live in a culture totally different from our own, a living that was stifling me. I could leave with a seeking heart.

I had not been going to church for several months, mainly because I was bored. Bored with getting up, sitting down, singing, all on cue like puppets, perfunctory prayers, and chitchat with people after church, where you already knew what would be said.

I knew I needed a spiritual renewal, a reawakening of the inner life, an enlightenment, so to speak. I kept these feelings to myself as the days stretched into months.

In the end I was agreeable to leaving all behind and taking what was for me a great step into the unknown. Now in this vehicle roaring down a real road in Nigeria, I wonder if my decision was right.

I look at the land on either side of the highway, dry earth that stretches into distances covered with scrubby brush and straggly trees. The sun is veiled by heavy brownish wisps of clouds. Reddish dust swirls and rolls across the road in front of us. Like the dust, my thoughts of the past whirl away and an increasing tide of excitement takes over as we pass white-robed men walking on the sides of the road and in the ditches. Loose tunics blow out from the men's bodies as they walk and the women's hips sway, wrapped tightly in bright cloth skirts.

We are on the road leading to the Baptist Girls' School at Abeokuta, which we must reach by nightfall. Thomas High says there are armed bandits on the highway after dark. He warns us that all drinking water must be filtered or we can get worms that will damage our livers. He tells us about the spitting cobra, green and black mambas, and other poisonous snakes in Nigeria. I freeze inside myself but feel sweat around my head and eyes. The fumes from the petrol cans beside me are nauseating.

We get in a traffic congestion at 8:00 P.M. and do not move for one-and-a-half hours. Swirling dust rides in the air, and women pass us balancing large pans of peeled oranges on their heads. Candle flames light the insides of small tin-roofed shacks along the highway.

I think of the word "hell" over and over. High starts the jeep engine again after it stalls, and we bump over ruts in the road, going slower, while pink or green colored taxis swerve by on either side. A truck backs into us, but nothing is damaged. We drive finally onto the main highway and after another hour turn into the gate at the women's school. All the buildings and grounds are in total darkness. There has been a power failure, something that happens often in Nigeria, due to a lack of trained technicians in this country, High tells us.

We find the home of Miss Elizabeth Truly, who directs the work and teaches here. In her we find a kind, round-faced, gray-haired woman in her sixties, who has been in this country for forty years and is retiring next year. She steps outside her house carrying a flashlight, called a torch in Nigeria, to light our way from the car to the house. She explains that a large truck parked nearby has brought water because of a water shortage. All this and Miss Truly lights a candle in the room where we are to sleep and invites us to come for a meal on a screened porch, as calmly and graciously as though presiding over a well-run, efficiently-functioning inn. By candlelight we eat a supper of pork chops, rice, fresh pineapple, green beans, ice tea, and boiled custard. I cannot believe there is food like this to eat after the brutal trip we've had to get here. I learn that a supply of food, some of it brought in from the States, is kept stocked for guests.

Once we are in bed, the night is full of strange noises outside. The darkness is so total—no lights shine anywhere. I lie thinking of the turbaned countenances I had glimpsed from the car window as we passed them along the roadside. There were splendid figures of men carrying themselves with dignity and style, their faces reflecting enigmatic and proud looks. The afternoon sun and dust seemed to pour without mercy over the land and the people, but life was being lived in spite of the harsh circumstances.

Tuesday, January 10th

I awake at 5:30 A.M., crying from an exhaustion that frays my emotions and thinking of the dreadful four-hour drive we will have this day to Ogbomosho, our final destination. Breakfast on the pleasant porch of Miss Truly's house helps restore me somewhat. Price, as usual, is serene and full of good cheer. Golden mangoes hang like jewels from the trees in the yard. The day is early and already hot. I take my time eating sweet rolls and drinking coffee. I am attempting to delay the trip.

But soon enough we are in the jeep and on the two-lane highway. The macadam road starts breaking up. Large hunks of the surface have been worn away, so we must drive around the holes. Burned out and wrecked cars are left in ditches where wrecks occur—there is no car towing or ambulance service. These grim reminders of twisted and scarred metal wrecks do not slow the traffic. There is no speed limit in Nigeria. We go swiftly by a landscape changing from low, scrubby brush land into jungles of tall banana plants, papaya plants, and towering skinny palms. We pass rusty, tin-roofed trading places piled with mangoes, pineapples, bananas, and yams. A number of people are cooking food in pots over open fires, while others dip into the pots with bowls, then use their fingers to eat the food.

Usually I am full of questions when we travel, but in this place I am speechless—I can only stare in disbelief at what I am seeing, experiencing, and feeling. Truly I am having culture shock. I recall reading about Isak Dinesen and her trek from an aristocratic home in Denmark to Kenya in the early part of this century. I need her fortitude. She was ill with malaria soon after her arrival but wrote letters to family and friends of her great life. Later, of course, disasters complicated her existence, yet she maintained an eternal love for Africa.

We stop for an hour in Ibadan at a building where Emmanuel Dahunsi, a Nigerian, and others work who are connected with the Baptist denomination in Nigeria. Dahunsi is general secretary of the Nigerian Baptist Convention. Dahunsi was formerly a student in Price's class at Southern Seminary in Louisville, Kentucky. He and his wife, Deborah, both from the Yoruba tribe, had come there from Nigeria around 1950 to study. He was admired as an able scholar and a winsome person. I remember well the day when the Kentucky Baptist Hospital in Louisville refused to admit Deborah Dahunsi because she was black.

Five hours after leaving Abeokuta, we reach Ogbomosho where we are to live and work. The town has the same primitive look of dirt, pot-filled roads leading off from the main highway, rusting tin-roofed shacks, mud houses, and people, people everywhere I look.

The seminary compound is like an oasis apart from the town. In the 1890s, when Baptist missionaries first established this place, lemon, lime, and orange trees were planted. Bougainvillea and frangipani trees bloom in shades of orange, purple, white, salmon pink, and rose. The buildings for administration, classrooms, and chapel are built in a traditional Southern United States style architecture—columns in front and a steeple on top of the chapel—all painted white. Covered walkways extend along the front of two buildings, one on each side of the central chapel. Grass grows around the buildings, along with numerous palm trees. A dusty road, bordered with towering teakwood trees, leads to dormitories and some faculty homes. Several original old mud buildings are still standing and in use. Flowering plants bloom in pots along walkways and open spaces. The faculty live in houses scattered here and there behind the main buildings, and the students and their wives occupy dormitories nearer the classrooms.

Tom High says that there has been no rain in Ogbomosho since last October and water in the town reservoir is running low. The potted plants are kept watered, but the grass is turning brown, and the palm trees look withered. By March the rains will begin and the grass will turn green.

Carl Whirley, the seminary president or principal, as he is called here in deference to British style, and Enid, his wife, come from the administration building to meet and welcome us. The Whirleys, both in their sixties, sturdily but not heavily built, smile at us with steady, happy eyes. I like them both instantly—no pretense, no airs. Kindness illumines their faces. We go to their home for lunch and enter a bungalow house of the type built in the early 1900s in the States.

They insist we rest after lunch. I am travel weary and bone tired and fall gratefully on the bed in the guest bedroom. We are to spend our first night here at the Whirley's house. At the foot of the bed is a blanket. Enid says I may need it before morning, but I find that difficult to believe. Then again, so many things have been beyond belief this day. On the twin bed opposite mine, Price is already snoring.

This morning we eat a breakfast of ripe, yellow papaya, (called pawpaw), eggs, and toast, and drink coffee with the Whirleys. I slept last night like someone drugged. Carl and Enid smile and are full of good cheer. While we eat and talk, we ask Carl to tell us some facts about Nigeria. He says that Nigeria is officially known as the Federal Republic of Nigeria. It has 900,000 square kilometers of land that stretch from the Atlantic Ocean to the Sahara Desert and more than eighty million inhabitants. He says no country has been more explored, visited, exploited, developed, administered, loved, and feared by foreigners.

We want to know about the geographical lay of the land. Carl tells us that behind the coastal strip of Nigeria is a belt of rain forest, forests dot the middle, and the East is the home of oil palms. North of the forest region, the savannah takes over with the land rising to central high plains. Ogbomosho is in the region known as "up country," bushland, at the edge of savannah country.

He points out that the British appeared in Nigeria in the seventeenth and eighteenth centuries as commercial traders and later as slave traders. After 1807, most of the British who came for the next one hundred years were explorers, traders, or missionaries. Finally, in 1960, Nigeria gained independence. It became a Republic in 1963. In 1966 the Federal Military government divided the country into twelve states in order to give a greater voice to smaller ethnic groups fearful of domination by larger groups. Sad to say, Carl reports there have been a number of assassinations of heads of state. Nigeria is presently under a military government headed by Lieutenant General Olesegun Obasanjo.

Enid tells us that we will move into a house on the compound left vacant by a single woman missionary on furlough.

An older man is in Enid's kitchen cooking, and a younger one serves us at the table. Enid introduces us to the men. From where I sit at the large table in the living room, I can see into one end of the kitchen where there is a seven-foot-long freezer, looking like a coffin. Enid says she goes to Ibadan, two hours' drive away, to a small supermarket for groceries and frozen food. She takes an ice chest along to bring food for the freezer. Coffee, especially, has to be hoarded when it is found to buy.

I think of having to travel on the highway again and push the thought from my mind. I concentrate on what is to be done tomorrow—getting settled in the house, unpacking our clothes, getting clothes washed, finding groceries. Enid tells me there is a washing machine in the house where we will live, but it doesn't work. She will get Nat, a Nigerian washerman who washes for her, to come and wash our clothes once a week. This is not inexpensive. We are to pay Nat the equivalent of eight dollars (US) per week.

I am disconcerted seeing and knowing of nationals here working for the mission people. Then I tell myself they are treated well and are paid fairly, better than other jobs might be for them. So how can this be wrong? Yet somehow I feel it is still the old master/servant relationship that establishes inequality immediately. Practiced for years by the British in Nigeria, the nationals are accustomed to it. Is it possible to develop a brotherhood of man where master/servant roles are understood? Surely, the mission, of all places, must be where this brotherhood occurs!

This afternoon I get acquainted with lizards—two or three small ones darting across the floor, up the wall, grayish-black in color, fast-moving. Enid and Carl drive us over to the four-bedroom house on the compound where we are to live. The house is a cream-colored stucco bungalow type, not the faded-red mud house construction of some of the older houses or buildings. I am happily surprised when we step inside. The rooms are large with many windows, the floors of wood, the furniture comfortable early American style. There is a gas stove and refrigerator and wall cabinets for dishes. We are going to live in a traditional sort of house.

We are sitting down to talk when out of the corner of my eye I see a small lizard dart across the floor and run up the wall. I jump up, clutching my skirts and yell, "Oh, Lord, there's a lizard in this house."

Enid laughs and looks calmly at me. "Don't worry, they won't hurt you."

"They!" I exclaim. "How many are there in the house?"

"Lizards are good at catching flies and ants. They really are good to have around. You'll see lots of them."

I sit down in silence. I continue to watch for the lizards, feeling like one is nearby ready to run up my leg. After Carl and Enid leave, I cry out, "Price, I can't live in a house with lizards."

16

"They're not going to hurt you. They're probably scared of you."

"How do you know that?"

"Well, no one here has been bitten or been hurt by one. They're small and harmless."

"But if they can run up walls, they could run on the ceiling and drop on our bed when we're asleep."

"Oh, come on, I doubt that. You're letting your imagination run away with you, aren't you?"

"Maybe so." I begin to calm down but keep a wary eye out for the lizard.

Late afternoon, I open the back door to go outside and immediately two large black, orange, and red lizards, with tails lashing, dart away from my feet. I yell, "Oh, come look at these lizards." To my amazement, I find the creatures a dazzling sight. How long these animals have been on this earth! Longer than man! I am reminded of Thoreau's admonition: "Do not despair of life. Think of the fox, prowling in a winter night to satisfy his hunger. His race survives; I do not believe any of them ever committed suicide."

Thursday, January 12th

Last night at 10:30 P.M., the big generator on campus knocked off and all the lights went out. We were in total darkness. Price managed to find the torch, and we searched for matches and candles. After we lighted the candles in the living room, we sat listening to the night watchman rustling fallen teakwood leaves on the ground as he walked to the back porch. He was starting guard duty for the night, sitting in a chair on the porch. To the side and front of our house stand tall teak trees. It is the custom on the compound for a Nigerian hunter to guard the houses. I felt comfortable knowing this man was our guard. I went to sleep listening to our watchman whistling signals to the other watchmen on campus. The long, high whistling moves eerily back and forth. I wonder what these long-time hunters in the forests are saying to each other.

This morning we go to the first chapel service of the semester at the seminary. Smiling, friendly students and wives are there. I am greeted by the name of "mama" or "ma."

17

Afterwards I go with Marjorie Stephens, who directs the women's work, to the Women's Building, a large, old mud house. Marjorie is an energetic, no-nonsense person. She is rather small, dark-haired, with her complexion tanned by years in the African sun. She is also in charge of the kitchen and of housekeeping at the Frances Jones house on campus, where we have arranged to eat our daily evening meal. This house is where Marjorie and Martha Gilliland, gynecologist and obstetrician at the Baptist Hospital here, live permanently. The hospital is across the road from the seminary and is staffed by Baptist doctors and Nigerian personnel. Guests of the seminary, here on brief visits, stay at Frances Jones, as well as persons from other countries coming to be patients at the hospital. I sensed immediately how difficult it would be to obtain food in Ogbomosho. I am delighted to have a place where we can pay for one good meal each day and eat in pleasant surroundings. A real boost to our morale!

On the way to the mud building, Marjorie tells me about how these mud houses were built and are still being constructed by Nigerians. A traditional mason lays three layers of mud balls a day. These dry hard and are smoothed over with fresh mud which acts as a mortar. Mud houses on campus are finished inside with painted walls and have wood floors. In villages, there may be dirt floors inside and no painted walls. This type house is cooler than one made of concrete blocks and is comfortable inside.

We talk about how poor the student wives are and how much they need. Workers in Marjorie's department teach the women how to use a sewing machine, how to cook on a stove indoors, and how to keep their children healthy. The wives are also taught English and Bible. Marjorie tells me that, at last year's graduation, the women jumped up and down with joy because they each received measuring spoons and cups, and muffin tins as gifts. So little makes them happy. A boiled egg each day, a piece of fruit— the Women's Department tries to provide a supplement to their poor diets. Sadly, Marjorie reports that the women do not like to practice birth control. They believe "the Lord will provide" no matter how many children they have.

What can ever change this attitude? I wonder. There is no easy solution to the problem. Children are insurance for their old age, a sort of Nigerian equivalent of Social Security. So many children die at a young age from malnutrition and a variety of diseases.

Having many children guarantees there will be someone around to care for parents in old age. Should we Westerners try to change the Nigerians' belief about this security and their way of life? The question nags at me. Already I see how affectionate student parents are with their children. There is a beauty in this love for children that the foreigner may be unwise in seeking to alter.

The day wears on under the bright, hot sun. I walk to our house down the worn path from the old mud building to the dusty road, then take a shortcut past two large cacti. I hear rustling of leaves underneath and hurry past looking behind scared that it is a snake.

I see Moses, the young gardener who is cultivating a vegetable garden in back of our house, leaning over, digging in the earth. He uses a short, short hoe and is bent double there, his head barely showing. He comes at daybreak every day except Saturday and Sunday, works until noon, then lies down for an hour or so on the ground under the shade of a large cashew tree. Every day he places the hoe and a machete in a storage room under the water tank next to our house, then starts his walk homeward down the path back of our house.

Will I ever forget the vividness of this scene, this place, this time? I don't think so. It is etched in my mind as if someone has taken a red hot iron and drawn it on my consciousness. A haunting sense of the presence of God also comes again and again to me these days.

In so brief a time, I am struck by how closely one lives to the earth and to people here. With no telephone, no television, no morning newspaper, the world does not intrude as much. There is time to look into a person's face when we talk and to listen. Life is being pared down and becoming meaningful. I resolve more and more not ever again to let time be frittered away by distractions.

T. S. Eliot called God "the still point of the turning world." I believe that I am being pointed toward that "still point."

Friday, January 13th

I am slow in moving this morning. The heat and change of climate is the cause. The body takes time to adjust to dramatic changes. I walk to the chapel for the student prayer retreat. Stu dents, wives, and children fill the pews. I watch how the women place and carry their babies on their backs. The woman bends or stoops over, takes the child and slides him on his stomach onto the flat part of her back, then ties a long piece of strong cloth around the baby, tying the front two ends around her stomach. A stronger, narrower piece of cloth is wrapped around the first cloth. All is done quickly and expertly. Babies fit neatly into the cloth pocket and seem happy there. They either sleep or look around wide-eyed, as cute as squirrels peeking from their nests.

We go to the Highs' house for lunch, walking through the backyard past lime, grapefruit, and avocado trees. The limes and grapefruit are ready to eat, and on our return homeward we stop to gather an armload. We hear the sound of African music, with its steady rhythm of drums and a tone like tin on tin being struck, coming from a house where a Nigerian faculty member lives. The dusty road covers our shoes with a fine film of soft, pale, creamy powder resembling talcum powder.

Once in our house I fall in bed, heavy-eyed from fatigue, and sleep for three hours. Price rests but has returned to his office when I awake. Tonight we are invited to eat with Bill and Alice Gaventa. Tall, with hair the color of salt and pepper, Bill is a quiet, gently-talking man. He has a look of understanding in his eyes, and you know you could trust him as your doctor. He is the Medical Director of the Baptist Hospital here. Alice has taken us under her wing like a mother hen with chickens. Alice is a person one instinctively likes. She lives to do for others. Willowy slim, her eyes and smile light up her face like no make-up could do. She helps us find food we need and brings us goodies to eat from time to time—like mango applesauce, guava jelly, corn muffins, cookies, and homemade bread.

After dinner we attend the seminary evening prayer retreat. One student is in front of the chapel on the platform telling about his half brother who is a wizard or witch doctor. Once the student was beaten severely by his brother. All this because the student chose to become a Christian. The more he talks the more animated he becomes. His dark eyes, burning and flashing, rivet your attention. His arms wave wildly in the air as he describes the evil brother. He speaks of how he tried to pray for this brother but believed himself under a spell that he could not break. Finally he was able to leave the area where his family and the brother live, never to return.

I am as spellbound as if a magician were performing on stage. Yet I know this has truly happened in the life of this student and of others. In reality it is the age-old struggle of good versus evil. These students are only an edge away from their tribal beliefs that have been a part of their lives for so long. They sometimes face persecution when they become Christians and enroll in the seminary to study. Some dare not ever return to their families in the villages. How difficult this would be to do; not many Christians would pay that price. They tell these stories joyously, seeming happy over the choice they have made.

Saturday, January 14th

After a breakfast of pawpaw and some plain yogurt, I wash my hair. Dust covers everything here, invading my hair. I must wash it often.

Enid drives by to take me to a grocery store in Ogbomosho. The small tin-topped wood shack fits into place along the main streets with other such shacks. Inside, African music is playing loudly on a radio and two or three young people are swaying and dancing to the music. Raucous talking goes on between the youths and the storekeeper. I look at the shelves containing medicine, cough syrup, throat lozenges, palm oil for cooking, powdered milk, rice, cider, wine, an orange drink, tomato paste, chocolate drink, cornstarch, soap, toothpaste, dried beans. All staples—not any fresh produce. I buy a box of cornflakes.

We leave and drive to another small store, where we find bleach, two cans of soup, and spaghetti, and we enquire about onions. A small girl runs outside, disappears, and brings back onions, along with some oranges.

We look outside and see a gray and red fire truck pulling up next door. A fire has started in a shack. People run excitedly to view the commotion. The fire is quickly contained.

A big Land Rover and a white car stop in front of the grocery store. Three robust men and two plump, frowzily-dressed women get out. They begin talking in English to Enid and to me. They are Russians living on the outskirts of Ogbomosho in a housing village of their own fabrication. They tell us they are from Moscow and are in Nigeria to install an oil pipeline. They want to know where we are from and where we live in Ogbomosho. We answer each other's questions in quick short words. They eye us curiously, as we do them. Soon they get into their cars and leave, honking noisily as they back into the road. I think, how strange that my first meeting and talking with Russians occurs in a bush country town in West Africa.

During all this commotion, a hen and her five chicks continue to scratch lazily on the ground, black and white goats frolic across the road, a man washes clothes in a pot back of the store, men on motorcycles whir by, and a woman is selling dried fish from a pan balanced on top of her head. I am entertained in a way I never am at home when I go for groceries. None of the noise, the confusion, the litter, or the foreign visitors disturbs the Nigerians. They seem to have the ability to absorb it all and continue in their customary ways—a dignified and courteous people.

Sunday, January 15th

I am awake at 5:00 A.M. this day, listening to unaccustomed sounds that take precedence over sleeping. Angry bird calls, shuffling of teakwood leaves, then a silence as profound as the darkness outside. Earlier I heard the throbbing drum beats that often wake me in the night. The steady sound continues, then stops abruptly. Another drum begins a different beat in answer to the first one. These are the talking drums used by the Yoruba in celebration of marriages, at times of death, or on festival days.

Sometimes the drums talk for important announcements or sound out praise poetry for important persons. The principle of the talking drum, an iya-ilu, relies on the fact that Yoruba is a tone language in which the meaning of the word depends partly on the speech tones. The pitch lines produced by the drum follow as closely as possible the tonal and rhythmic patterns of spoken texts.

After the drums quiet, often far off I begin to hear a rhythmical chanting or ecstatic singing. I look at the clock and see that the time may be 2:00 or 3:00 A.M. I lie in bed, staring out the narrow window next to my bedside, fully expecting to see some figure dancing outside, clothed only in animal skins and carrying a spear. The strong smell of earth warmed by the heat of the day mingles with the night music. The darkness outside is alive with a mystery that stirs my blood.

Sure enough, the electricity is off, as Carl predicted it might be today. I take the torch from the bedside table and move noiselessly through the living room to the kitchen. After I find matches and a candle, I sit in a chair by a window, waiting for dawn, believing I am no stranger to God. What are we for, here or anywhere? I ask myself. Through our work we are shaping ourselves and those whose lives we touch, I am convinced. Hopefully, we do this with thoughtfulness and care and love.

It is a Sunday morning here and we will attend our first church service at Antioch church, where students and faculty worship. On the dusty road walking to church, we meet with students, their wives, and children. I don't want to stare but am fascinated by the bright-colored material the wives wear in long skirts and blouses, and as turbans on their heads. Heavy reddish-brown dust is everywhere, yet everyone is clean and freshly attired. Once in church, I watch the well-behaved children. So many babies, too, fat and lively with dark expressive eyes. The girl babies wear tiny gold earrings in their ears. Mothers hold them close and not one cries.

Monday, January 16th

We are up at 6:00 A.M. and no lights. We eat cornflakes by candlelight. I cut up the small bananas that I bought yesterday from the young trading woman who came to the back door. She carried a pan of bananas on her head and her baby strapped to her back. She asked me for food for the baby. I had nothing a small baby could chew but a slice of bread, which I gave the mother. She smiled and broke off pieces to give her sweet-eyed child.

Last night Martha suggested we mix brewer's yeast in water and take every day to keep up our energy. The taste is like wet earth on my tongue this morning. We have to remember also to take anti-malaria tablets daily. In spite of taking these tablets, some of the mission people have bouts with malaria.

The sky lightens into dirty gray outside. Moses comes walking barefoot down the path to begin his day's work. My day begins when I see Moses arrive. He is Africa to me. Short and slight of frame, not a spare ounce of fat on his body, he always wears trousers and a tunic, once white but now stained with the soil in

23

which he works. He doesn't stroll along but comes quickly and determined in demeanor to his job. At no time is there anyone in the garden to be his boss, but he hoes or plants and watches over this place the day long, except for rest at noontime. He wears no watch to tell him when it is 5:00 P.M., but promptly at that time each day he leaves. From the back windows of the house I can glimpse his figure, steady and unperturbed, one with the earth and the sky. Yes, Moses is a survivor in a land that can eat up a human being as does a wild animal. I admire him. He helps me not to feel as isolated in this new environment as I sometimes feel in my own house on a suburban street. I am grateful for this feeling of nearness to him and he to me when I go outside and, smiling, he hands me a newly-ripe pawpaw.

Gloria, wife of a seminary student named David, comes today to begin helping me with housework once a week to earn money. She is the mother of three living children and one dead child. Her name suits her well. Short and small-boned, wiry and quick in movement, she radiates toothy smiles and cheer. She is a second year student at the Women's Building and speaks English well enough for us to communicate. Mid-morning I offer Gloria a cold glass of milk to drink, which she leaves on the table until it is warm before drinking it. Nor will she eat anything cold from the refrigerator. I often wonder what Moses eats for lunch and would give him food, but Nigerians seem not to like our food. When Gloria leaves for her place, I give her onions and tomatoes which she can use in cooking.

This afternoon I talk with one of the faculty members about my teaching an evening writing class for the men. The men need training in a journalistic style of writing, he says. I doubt many of them will do that kind of writing, but I am willing to try and teach them from my background of newspaper work. I taught journalism and did the publicity for a college in Texas years ago. I have no textbooks of my own here. A few helpful books are in the seminary library, I am told. Most of the teaching will have to come out of my head.

Late in the day I meet Price at his office, and we walk back to our house together down the now familiar dusty path. The frangipani tree is in glorious bloom—white blossoms with salmon-colored streaks inside. The scent is heavy and sweet. Everything seems in excess in this place. I feel exhausted in mind and body from the heat today.

Tuesday, January 17th

I am awake at 5:30 A.M. when the light outside begins to quickly appear. The morning breaks clear and fine. I make coffee and write two letters. I get down on my hands and knees, working to get the oven lighted in the old gas stove in our kitchen. I have no luck and neither does Price when he tries later in the morning.

I go to the Women's Building to observe the teaching of an English class to the student wives. I am to begin teaching English there day after tomorrow. While I sit in the old mud house with its open windows and doors (no glass, no screens), I am overcome with a strange and eerie feeling. Suddenly I am thrown off balance and dizzy with wondering where I am, so far away from home. After a few minutes, I am back to the reality of the classroom.

Shirley Gunn comes to show me how to light our oven. Shirley, seminary librarian, is a young, single woman who lives alone in the house next door to ours. She has as a companion a dachshund that stays indoors but likes to sneak out early mornings and bark at the women who scoop up teakwood leaves in our yard. The women soak these dry leaves in water and use them to wrap produce for marketing.

I wash lettuce bought yesterday from a trader woman—the first lettuce I've seen here and it is grown on a farm, Shirley says. I dislike washing it in bleach but know this is necessary to kill any germs. A chemical taste lingers on the lettuce.

Wednesday, January 18th

There was lightning in the sky last night as I left the classroom building where I teach writing to nine men students. All of the men are enthusiastic and interested, a joy to teach. They ask questions and get into heated discussions. One thing I am learning is that what tribe a man comes from matters. There is great loyalty to the tribe, to the name, to the language spoken.

Late this afternoon, how good to see dark clouds overhead for a change, instead of the usual dull sky that lingers around the sun. During the day the sun moves lazily across the top of the sky. I look forward to evenings when billions of stars hover close above me wherever I gaze. No neon lights here to outdo them, only a black sky and crowded stars, each one twinkling like newly-washed and polished fine crystal. And flung across the heavens is the trailing white scarf of the Milky Way, veiling more stars. If we watch closely, often we can see a shooting star.

The nearness of God pervades my being standing under these stars. We need a relationship with creation that is natural and not forced. Life lived away from contact with earth's natural elements separates us from our Creator. I believe we ought to feel direct relationship with the world outside our limited boundaries, to leave the finite for the infinite. There are rare, marvelous times when this can and does happen. Stargazing in the tropical night is such an experience. I had forgotten the wonder of silence under the stars, looking and listening.

Rilke believed that in our time men ought to listen more, listen to the stars shining in the sky. He wrote: "Oh, if they spoke to us, the remotest, ancient, most ancient forbears! And we: listeners at last. The first human listeners." In a mystical way, stars do speak to me.

Thursday, January 19th

Today, I am to begin teaching English to the seminary students' wives. I wake up with a headache, nervous over meeting the women. I gather up my books and my courage and walk the short path from our house to the road that leads to the Women's Building under the teak trees. The air is pleasant today because of a rain in the night. There are only four of the original mud-constructed buildings on the campus. These were built in the late 1800s when the mission was established in Ogbomosho. What perils the mission people who came to this country then faced. Disease (no medicine to control malaria as at present), no electricity, no running water, and isolated without modern means of communication. Brave men and women to be sure. The once reddish-brown buildings have dried to a cocoa brown color and blend with the landscape harmoniously. In the towns and villages these mud houses continue to be built. I hope they don't disappear.

The classroom has four rows with five desks in each row of the old-fashioned kind, a seat and a desk-part connected to the seat. These must have come from the US.

A young woman sits at one of these desks, cradling a dark-eyed, smiling baby whose mahogany-colored skin matches his mother's. I say "Hello," not knowing whether this woman can understand me. She nods, and cautiously, I ask, "Is this your first baby?" thinking how very young she looks.

"No, mum, my seventh," she answers slowly in English and with no sign of emotion.

"Oh" I smile, trying not to show surprise in my face.

Then I look into her weary eyes and ask, "How many boys and how many girls?"

And she calmly replies, "seven boys, mum."

"And what is your name?" I want to know.

"Patience, mum," comes the same calm, low reply.

What a marvelous name for you, I think to myself. From that time on, Patience and I are special friends and Benjamin, her seventh son, six months old, comes to class with her daily.

Other women begin to drift slowly and timidly into the classroom, until there are ten students in all. They watch me curiously. I look at them in their floor-length, tight, flowered skirts and blouses, some with their heads wrapped in scarves. How far away home is this morning. I am a stranger in a strange land.

I begin by introducing myself and telling them about where I am from and about my family, my husband, three children, and four grandchildren, with another grandchild to be born in May. When I talk of my grandchildren, their eyes widen and several women make a sound of "Oh, Oh."

I am impressed by their warmth of spirit when I talk of my family. Already I am aware of the deep bond of love between Nigerians and their children. Mothers carry their children close to their bodies until the babies are a year or more old. A father will proudly tell you of his family, nuclear and extended. This sense of the extended family group is at the heart of these people's relationship with each other. Although the infant mortality rate is high (one out of ten children does not live to the age of ten), couples continue to believe that a large family ensures that there will always be an elder brother to look after the parents and others.

Four different tribal languages are spoken among this small group of ten women. Most of them speak a smattering of English but need to improve their speaking, writing, and reading skills. I sense that there are ten distinct personalities in this room. One looks shy and reserved, another withdrawn, one haughty and cool, and over by the window is one who is full of energy and talk. I have a feeling that this will be a good group to teach. I relax, pass out books which are like first-grade readers, and begin the first lesson. Although the door and two windows are wide open to the outdoors, the temperature in the room seems one hundred degrees. When a bell rings at 10:00 A.M., I welcome the sound. We part company, nodding and smiling to each other at the classroom door.

Friday, January 20th

So much sharing goes on here. Last night, Ruth Womack, who directs the work for malnourished mothers and babies at Kersey Home, located outside the town, gave me a pair of socks to wear inside my shoes, when we are out walking. Hazel Moon, who is in charge of the Health Service for treatment of Hansen's disease (once called leprosy) near Ogbomosho, brought by for us a jar of sugared peanuts, called groundnuts. This week we are having soup, bread, and yogurt that Alice prepared. How can I ever repay these generous-hearted people? I do not believe they expect you to do so. It is not a question of you do for me, then I must do for you. Out of the little they have, they share happily.

I nap in the afternoon, thinking, too, about the English class tomorrow. This morning in class we laughed together about the difference in words for "face" and "hands" in their language and in English. But I wonder how much I will be able to help these women learn the necessary English for good communication. In the US, we are spoiled with expecting praise when we do something for others. Too often we need to be thanked so we, in turn, can feel righteous and good.

Tomorrow we are going to Oshogbo, a town nearly an hour's drive from Ogbomosho. We must be officially registered as aliens in this country, a government requirement. Mofeku, a driver for the seminary, will take us there and back in the sturdy Peugeot, the preferred car here because it holds up in bad road conditions. The drive will be over a road of washed-out gullies and big potholes. Yet it will mean a chance to see the countryside of small villages and the terrain of savannah and forests. Passing along the roadside where women pound cassava in wooden, bucket-like mortars with long, wooden pestles and where scantily-clad children, some naked, chase each other in play, is a long way from Main Street, USA. How little contact these people have with the outside world. I like the thought of entering these places, seemingly removed from time.

As the poet Dylan Thomas expressed it, time seems to hold us "in chains." We think that where we live and move and have our being is the only time. To see a land where people live in an innocence and amid a rawness of nature that is primitive is to know time past.

And like Rilke thought, "we of the here and now are not for a moment hedged in the time-world, nor confined within it; we are incessantly flowing over and over to those who preceded us, to our origins and to those who seemingly come after us." We are a part of all we meet.

Saturday, January 21st

After breakfast at daylight, Mofeku comes to get Price and me for the drive to Oshogbo. He speaks little English and is a small, slender man wearing a tunic and trousers of bright orange, a soiled Muslim-type cap on his head, and a pair of child-sized sunglasses, rimmed in white.

We bounce and jostle on the road. I hold tight to a rod above the door on my right, but still I rise from the seat and plop back again when the right wheel falls into potholes. No one says anything. Here you do not complain or exclaim about inconveniences or extraordinary circumstances. Mofeku is a good driver. He is expert at dodging motorcycles and lorries that bear down on us from the opposite direction. We pass matted vegetation, green and lush giant leaves on trees and vines, mud houses clumped together in villages, one large Anglican church, and a school where the children in blue and white uniforms run to the roadside, waving to us. Farther on, naked children play in the dirt around clusters of straw-thatched huts.

Coming into Oshogbo, known as an art colony or center, we see tin-roofed stores advertising a bank, fashion house, barbers' provisions, and a book shop. But not one resembles such places in our country. Wood shacks are crowded together under tin roofs, small and cramped inside, where dirt streets lead to them.

We go to the official police headquarters, are told to sit in a small bare room stifling with heat and wait. A young uniformed man appears in thirty minutes, looking angry and harassed. He has us fill out some papers, glances over them, says nothing, leaves, comes again, and has us fill out more papers. After another long wait, he returns our alien registration card, which we must turn back to his office when we leave Nigeria in May. Then it is into the Peugeot and the long grueling ride to Ogbomosho.

Sunday, January 22nd

I was a long time going to sleep last night, not worrying or feeling badly, but encountering a restlessness hard to define. Maybe it is what Wordsworth in "Tintern Abbey" means when he writes about the "sad, still music of humanity." I am disturbed over the sea of humanity in this country, the ever-increasing birth rate, and not enough food or decent housing for the majority. I remember the sad eyes of thin women sitting in front of huts in the heat of day. Where do they find the will to survive? Yet the suicide rate in Nigeria is not high. I am told that people are arrested and put in jail for trying to commit suicide and are told by the judge that they must learn to face problems, that this is a part of life.

There is a reverence for life here that is difficult to describe. You see it in peoples' respect for the elderly and in their love of children. Students speak and bow slightly from the waist when they pass me on campus or in the classroom building. At first a woman in my class would stand to speak when I asked her a question. A holdover from British days of rule, I suppose. I told the women there was no need to do this and to remain seated.

Yesterday I learned that one of every four Africans south of the Sahara live in Nigeria and that one percent of the population controls 75 percent of the nation's wealth. Life expectancy is 39 years, even in 1978, and the literacy rate is barely 30 percent. And there are 250 ethnic groups within this country!

I am learning a few Yoruba words. Words are often repeated two or three times for emphasis. It is "hot, hot," or your dress is "fine, fine," or follow me "now, now!" Very expressive.

It would seem that everyone in this town is a woman trader or seller of goods or produce. There is a saying here that "if you have two of something, you sell one." These women traders begin by selling from door to door, carrying their produce or wares on pans or baskets atop their heads. A heavy, round pad of cloth goes on the head first to help balance the load. Gradually they accumulate enough money to start a business—a store where they sell cloth or groceries. Apparently, a woman trader can become wealthy in time.

Monday, January 23rd

Plodding with one foot in front of the other one today. Not moving easily. I am looking this morning for some color in the sunrise. None appears. Price leaves to go with Carl, driving to Ilorin for a meeting. He will be gone until late afternoon. Monday and no English class today. I walk to the seminary's small library and look at the Nigerian newspaper published in Lagos. In it is a strange assortment of stories, but the weirdest feature is the printing of large pictures of the deceased persons of that day on five full pages of the paper.

Slowly I walk to our house thinking of what I will eat for lunch. Enid comes later to invite me to eat with her at her house. From her big freezer she brings out sliced beef, lima beans, and banana nut bread.

Enid tells me of coming by ship to Africa in 1950 and of the hardships encountered after arriving here. She has a philosophy of making the best of everything, based on her solid faith in God's providence. Her calm presence is relaxing. After lunch, we sit in comfortable chairs in her living room, under a ceiling fan, and talk about our children far away. It does us both good, this "women talk."

I leave and walk to our house by way of the traveler's palm, shaped like a huge green fan, and farther on by a mango tree loaded with mangoes turning from green to yellow. Weary from the heat and an unreasonable sense of isolation today, I decide to nap. I drift off to sleep hearing the scratching sound of Moses' hoe in his garden and the laughter of school children on the road in front of our house. I like going to sleep to such peaceful noises.

Tuesday, January 24th

Awakened by the dismal call of a bird, like someone striking a hammer on an anvil in steady rhythm. I wonder if it is the forlorn crying of the titihoya, a bird that Alan Paton wrote about in *Cry the Beloved Country*.

The cry stops at daybreak. By candlelight I cook some bacon that Enid brought me from her trip to the Ibadan store.

All the women look sleepy-eyed this morning in English class. I feel sorry for them. They have to get up early, cook breakfast, take care of three to eight children, wash clothes outside, walk to market and carry loads of produce home on their heads, and go to classes every day. Women usually defer to men and children and let them eat first. Mrs. Bobo, a Nigerian helper at the Women's Building, has three children and is pregnant again. Most mornings she can hardly hold up her head but sleeps with head lying on her folded arms across the desk. Marjorie is giving her vitamins. Price says he thinks the women are physically tired, not emotionally worn out. I wonder. A woman's emotional state of being can make her weary also.

The writing class this evening goes well. The men are motivated and anxious to learn, which makes teaching a pleasure. They also write better than I expected them to do. Price comes, after class, to walk with me in the dark night by the cactus bush where rats hang out. I am still a coward going past there by myself after dark. The slightest rustling of leaves can send me scurrying.

I depend so much on this man of mine. And, in his way, Price depends on me. D. H. Lawrence said "marriage should be where a man and woman, like two poles, hold the world between them."

Now, walking along with Price, I wonder aloud, "Where is the moon?" I miss seeing the moon in its various stages of unfolding. We see more often the golden full moon.

"Watch where you are going," Price suddenly warns me.

I am so busy looking overhead that I almost walk into a cactus bush. Its sharp, saw-like edges brush my legs.

I veer toward the frangipani tree, wanting to bury my face in its sweet scent, calling to Price to come do the same. He is more intent on getting to the house for a cup of coffee, but he comes and lifts one velvet blossom to sniff.

"Oh, my, that's powerful," he exclaims, and wonders what other flower smells like that.

"I think it's the tube rose," I answer.

I continue thinking about flowers because the growing and caring for flowers has always been so much a part of my life. One of the loveliest memories I have of my dear mother is of her standing one spring afternoon, wearing a purple linen dress, in the middle of her purple and white-blooming iris flower bed. Oh, memories, memories, how they color life.

I learned today that the dawn calling bird is a fruit bat. Now that the pawpaws are ripe, it is staying nearby. I like its steady, mournful call awakening me at daylight. I am put in touch with elemental things. These days in Africa I live closer to and am in contact with God-made creation instead of man-made. At the same time, I dig deeper into my inner self in relation to all this.

Wednesday, January 25th

I like our early morning rising. Eating breakfast by candlelight many mornings is a mind-relaxing time. The air is warm but not yet heated. Teakwood leaves rustle and fall from the big trees outside. There is a quietness, a hushed expectancy beyond the windows where dawn begins to break.

This morning I go to the Women's Building to see all the babies weighed and inoculated. Ruth Womack, a nurse, does the work of charting and weighing the children. The weighing contraption is a long hook hung on a scale, supported at each end by two rods, like a playground swing. Each baby is placed inside a pair of short overalls, then hung from a loop on the overalls to a hook on the scales. Most babies are fat and cute but some have protruding navels. The protrusion usually recedes when the child is three years old. One child has a necklace of blue glass beads around her small, naked bottom, possibly to ward off sickness.

Later Price and I go to chapel service. He attends faithfully every weekday morning. Today a male chorus sings, accompanied only by drums. The singers clap their hands, sing, and praise God in song. Several student speakers tell of their grandfathers who were cannibals and sacrificed children. Both the young men and the older students speak openly of their difficult past and of what a difference is felt in their lives at present.

In the Yoruba tribal beliefs, illness and death, except in the very old, are seen as evidence of ill will from the spirit world. Witchcraft, springing from envy and hate, brings misfortune. In every community, specialist practitioners exist to identify witches, to divine causes of illness and misfortune, and to prescribe treatment, sometimes magical, sometimes medicinal. These students have come from such a background to have an almost child-like faith and belief in God that runs deep, with no superficial showmanship or pretension or attempt to impress. Their words are heart-felt, humbly and gratefully spoken.

Weary from heat and a sense of longing for our home today, I decide to sleep in mid-afternoon. Price comes in before we are to go to Frances Jones. Out the door we go, across the front lawn to the public dirt road in front of our house. I believe that from somewhere at the end of this road comes the high-pitched singing and chanting I often hear in early morning hours. Price thinks I am mistaken. He says voices carry a long, long way when there is no other noise and suggests somewhere far off.

I long to see for myself if there could be a place of cult worship down the road. Price cautions me to be reasonable, saying we cannot penetrate such secret circles. So we turn toward the way that leads to Frances Jones, to the civilized dining room and diners, leaving the matted undergrowth and density of forest that lies mysteriously ahead. I linger, looking back expectantly.

Price regrets that we will miss the excitement of spring coming on, as it will be doing soon in South Carolina.

"Maybe I shouldn't be so enthusiastic about a change of seasons," he speculates.

"Oh, no," I quickly cry out. "Why not? We need to feel that way, to be filled with joy over the first crocus, the first jonquil. I think it's wonderful to be passionate about springtime and not take it for granted!"

"I suppose if we were all alive within ourselves and with God, nothing would seem ordinary," he concludes. His thought leaves me pondering, as it does so many times.

To our surprise, Sam, the cook at Frances Jones, has a luscious chocolate pie for dessert tonight, especially made for Price. He must have overheard our talk about missing good pies or Marjorie probably dropped the word to Sam. Anyway, it makes for an exciting evening, having a chocolate pie! My spirits lift and Price is all smiles. I go to the kitchen and thank Sam for the extra effort he made this day. A broad smile lights his face.

Thursday, January 26th

This morning I wrap a piece of bright cloth, brown with gold and red figured print, into a long skirt, Nigerian style, to wear to English class. I bought the fabric in Dakar, in Senegal, where we went shopping in the cloth market one afternoon.

The women from my class, and others, laugh and clap their hands when they see me coming. They gather in a long line down the narrow porch that fronts the classroom to shout and sing. There is a trick to wrapping the material around your waist so that it will not come apart. They did not believe I could do this and are delighted I succeeded.

In the afternoon we go to a mission prayer meeting at the Gaventas' house. I look forward to these meetings where everyone is much in prayer for many people. Here I listen to prayers from men and women who are putting their lives on the line for others. They practice daily what they believe in, what they confess with their words. The feeling at this prayer meeting is spiritual, a God-in-our-midst place.

We stay to eat supper by candlelight with the Gaventas in their back yard. Surprisingly, there are no mosquitoes or insects. Lizards are great repellents. We watch the stars puncture the sky and begin their nightly dancing.

Walking home, Price and I spy a full gold moon riding high in the heavens.

"There's your moon," Price is careful to point out.

"Yes, and isn't it glorious?" I muse. "Let's look our fill now before it disappears to sleep."

"For it was Shelley who wrote:
Thou art folded, thou art lying
In the light which is undying
Of thine own joy, and heaven's smile divine . . ."

I thank God for putting me in this place among these people whom I am learning to love.

Friday, January 27th

Where is the time going? A question I often ask myself. Days melt into one another when one has no sense of time. I seldom wear my watch during the day. I am aware sharply of night descending and light arriving in the morning. Other than those times, for once in my life, I do not have to live by the clock. The body slows down and looks and listens when time is no longer all-important.

Moses doesn't wear a watch, yet he arrives at the garden and leaves at the same time each day. I have never seen watches on any of the people in the villages we pass along the roadside. The Fulani, the nomadic tribe who wander with their cattle, have no watches or clocks that I can see. Time seems to be reckoned here by close attention to nature. As Wordsworth wrote, there is "A motion and a spirit, that impels all thinking things, all objects of thought, and rolls through all things." If only we could stay in touch with that motion and spirit. I love the Ibo tribe's proverb: "Let me in innocence wish you, as myself, a brimming pool from which leaking time cannot steal."

After breakfast I begin writing a story for the Greenville News. This story is my account of attending church services in a church in Ogbomosho that seats 2,000 people. Sitting there, I identified with feelings of the minority at home.

Price comes for lunch. I have by now learned to drink milk I make from powdered milk and filtered water. Alice told us not to eat any of the cashews falling ripe from the cashew tree in the back yard. She said that they contain a certain poison until they are roasted, in their shells, in a fire. Even the ashes from the fire are poisonous. What a parable of life. Sometimes something very good can be hidden in the worst of people, and it takes a refining fire to burn it out.

I cannot believe we have no mail yet from our children. I begin fretting. I have always been the letter writer in our family. Many men do not like to write personal letters, apparently. When I write I expect a reply. Price tells me not to start thinking something bad has happened. I have to be more patient, maybe another week. Patience is not one of my virtues, I'm afraid. However, the practice of patience is being thrust upon me.

After lunch, Price returns to his office to do some work. At the door, he turns and says playfully, "Be a good girl, now." He knows full well there aren't any temptations likely to occur here.

But I tease back and answer, "No, I think I'll take the next lorry (bus) to Timbuktu!"

Difficult to believe Timbuktu is perhaps only 1,000 miles to the northwest of Ogbomosho, a short distance from the Upper Niger River in Mali.

Saturday, January 28th

After breakfast this morning, Alice brings lime juice that I am to put in cold water at the morning break in the faculty lounge.

We sit and laugh together about some of the unusual signs in English at the rear of lorries on the highway. My favorite one is: "No Condition Permanent." Others I have seen are: "Behold the Bridegroom Cometh," "The Lord Is My Shepherd," "Watch Out, Watch Out, Don't Kiss Me, Watch Out," "Noah's Ark Never Tumbles," "Father Forgive Us," and "Sea Never Dry." They range from the ridiculous to the sublime. Alice says she has no idea where the ideas for the signs originate. Some businesses have humorous signs in front, such as: "God's Will Beer Parlor," "Suru Lere -Patience Is Rewarding," "Sweet Love and Trading Store," "Decency Hotel," "Happy Hotel." At one place with a sign, "Modern House of Fashion," over the doorway, goats bounded in and out the door, and a woman cooked food in a pot over a fire in the yard outside. The Hausa people have a way of saying to anyone starting on a journey: "May you come down (meaning from a camel) in peace." That is a lovely expression.

Later I walk to morning break carrying my jar of lime juice. Threads of rain begin to moisten my head and face. I walk slowly, taking time to feel the enveloping coolness. Everyone looks at me when I arrive at the lounge, soaked from head to feet. No matter, for I will be dry soon in this hot building. I concur with Emily Bronte who liked to walk where her own nature led her. The lime juice and water is refreshing. What a good beginning to this day!

Sunday, January 29th

Today we are to go with Carl and Enid to a pastor's conference in Oyo, a forty-five minute drive from Ogbomosho. Old Oyo long ago was the administrative capital of the once mighty Yoruba empire. The morning is hot and muggy, and there will be no coolness in car or building. We take bottles of filtered water to drink during the day. Each house on the mission compound has a filter attachment to its water faucet in the kitchen.

The highway teems with gasoline trucks, lorries, and only a few private cars. The truck and lorry drivers go at a high speed. They think nothing of passing on blind curves and over hills. A certain Islamic *kismet*, or fate, is at the wheel. I am exhausted from watching the dangers. I try to look at the countryside instead of the road.

We arrive at the Oyo Baptist Church, built of ugly gray concrete blocks. Inside, the long narrow benches have no backs. I look around at the varied group of people—students, some in Western style shirts and pants, other people in bright Nigerian dress, colors of pink, blue, orange, wine, and silver. The meeting is three hours long, with us sitting on hard seats. Men go to sleep and other men stroll the aisles waking them up by poking with long sticks. A few overhead fans whirl, then stop. I grow numb, my stomach growls, my head aches, and I feel my back crumpling. Price looks at me weary-eyed.

Finally we leave and go to a Nigerian pastor's small concrete block house for lunch. On the table are chicken with red hot sauce, mashed purple yams over which hot sauce is poured, and a slime-looking green soup, *efou*, made of a type of spinach. I cannot eat the *efou* and the chicken burns my mouth. Price eats everything but cannot manage the spinach. Dahunsi sits at our table and explains the food to us and asks for soda for us to drink. While we are eating, women and children are serving the eight of us around the table. They smile happily at us.

Riding home down the hazardous highway, I long to be back in our own house in the States, cooking food we like. Somehow this has been a difficult day. Yes, Americans and Nigerians are far apart in heritage and culture and there was no meeting of minds today that I could discern.

Monday, January 30th

A day I dread. We are to visit the Health Service and hospital on the outskirts of Ogbomosho. Hazel Moon directs the work there and has been in Nigeria for forty years. She goes with us this morning into the hospital ward where a few men with Hansen's disease are being treated. Some persons have no feet, or have fingers missing, or their faces half eaten away. Emotionally I know that I am seeing these sights, yet I seem not to be inside myself as I gaze at these disfigured people. They smile. Everything is clean. One man's feet have been saved because of hot wax treatments. Hazel says these treatments bring no pain to the patients. This man kicks his feet proudly and grins. The patients speak only Yoruba, so we cannot converse with them. Instead, we do a lot of smiling.

We drive to a bush village near the hospital. Patients must live outside the town and are considered outcasts by their families and villagers. One man in the patients' village has no feet but gets around on a small cart he's made with skate wheels on the bottom. An 80-year-old woman lives here who is blind, with no eyes in her eye sockets, and no fingers. Others in the village take care of her. Today some people are cooking yams and grinding cassava. Their small mud houses have thatched roofs. Later, we stop at Hazel's house several miles down the road, set back from a large yard of tangerine and mango trees that Hazel planted. She gives us cake and ice cream to eat, but I relish only a few bites.

We end the day visiting in the hospital in Ogbomosho. Bill Gaventa shows us the reception room where a mob of people, some standing, some sitting on benches and some on the floor, all wait to see a doctor. The place is clean and free of bad odors but looks old. Martha Gilliland shows us a new wing in the maternity ward with more modern hospital beds. She walks around the room, proud of this addition. Martha belies her 50-plus years. She walks and works with the energy of a 30-year-old and has the trim figure to match. She bicycles to and from the hospital.

Here the rooms look more like a hospital at home. Babies are placed in cribs next to the mother's bed. There is no kitchen in the hospital; families bring food to the patients and often water when there is a town water shortage.

Martha works miracles among the women patients. In this place, she is in her rightful milieu. Martha's smile and presence must surely comfort her women patients, many of whom were once treated by tribal medicine men.

Tuesday, January 31st

Up during the night fighting a mosquito. Found a big spider on the wall back of our bed. I am terrified. Price hits it with the bottom of a shoe, then we can't find it. We don't know if the thing is dead or not. We move to another bed which is not comfortable. I lie awake thinking of all the crawly things—snakes, lizards, rats, and spiders. How do the Nigerians sleep on dirt floors in their mud houses with such things around?

This morning I am sleepy, passive, dazed, wondering what I am doing here thousands of miles from home in dust and heat. I long to see clean yards, green grass, and familiar trees. A long nap in the afternoon helps my black mood. Price thinks a letter from the children would cheer me. He is so right. Seldom is he depressed.

FEBRUARY

Wednesday, February 1st

At dawn this morning I am up when the women begin gathering teakwood leaves outside. I cannot see them, but I know they are there by the tinkle, crackle sound of leaves being piled by hand into baskets they carry.

Baskets of leaves make easy work compared to the loads of firewood some women carry on their heads and backs. We are told that one day a man came to the Baptist Hospital, complaining of pain in his back. He said he hurt his back helping another man load a hundred pounds of firewood onto his wife's head!

February is in the midst of the *harmattan*, when northerly land winds blow fiercely from the Sahara, bringing the dust of the desert to sting the eyes and to cover everything with its thin, rose-red veneer. In late afternoon, the sun hangs low in the hazy sky before sliding suddenly over the horizon. Last night the moon looked shrouded in a gauze-like cloth, ghostly and unfriendly. The night air coming through the window labored forcibly in sharp gusts, not softly and timidly as on other evenings. I can sense a change coming in the weather—a feeling to be tuned to nature, so to speak. Here the violence of the sunshine, the closeness of stars at night, and the way we walk so intimately with earthy things makes me feel more alive, more whole.

I die daily here—my heart is moved by so many sights and scenes. This morning a young African woman comes to the door, her baby strapped to her back, yet she superbly balances a basket of eggplant and peppers on her head. I can never say "no" to these women traders. I would like to know them better.

The people, more than anything else, make the country so interesting. Whenever I look out the windows of this house toward the dusty road below our yard, I see movement. White uniformed school children in clusters of three or four, skipping and often singing, and women traders walking in that quick, graceful gait they adopt to balance the pans or baskets. Or here comes a woman with bananas, chewing on the Nigerian toothbrush, a long peeled stick in her mouth. I never tire of watching these scenes.

Tonight at Frances Jones, Martha is late for dinner but comes in looking calm and cool in a pretty flower-printed dress. Martha is on stage tonight. She overshadows Marjorie telling dramatic stories, or joking and laughing. She could have been an actress.

Then Martha reports we will have a new face at the dinner table soon. He is Lech Nowogrodski, a young Polish man in Nigeria to do land surveys for the Nigerian government. The government-run hotel in town is not acceptable to his standards. This news of a newcomer is exciting, and he speaks English, too!

Hazel Moon is a guest for dinner. She talks about our visit with the patients with Hansen's disease. Many visitors from the States to the seminary will not visit the colony, Hazel says, because they fear being shocked by what they might see. I tell her I felt such emotions also. It is difficult for Hazel to realize the patients are not whole people physically, having spent years among them. Later Price gives her money to help one of her patients.

We walk home guided by light from our torch, past the trees where lemons and grapefruit hang like small lanterns in the trees. I pull two grapefruit for our breakfast in the morning. Far off I hear the talking drums beating along with the ebb and flow of voices chanting a song. I am reminded of how this sad sound must have been heard often in the night long ago in the American South, when the slaves' work was done.

Passing under the trees, I think of snakes that are reported to drop down from tops of trees on a person below. I skitter away toward the known path. Price wants to know what's the matter with me.

"I thought there might be a snake up there," I answer, pointing to the tree. "Wait a minute, what is that whirring noise I hear?" "I don't hear a thing," he mutters in disbelief.

We move on toward the rear porch of our house. The night watchman is sitting there in an old, broken-down porch swing that creaks and whirs as it moves. He usually sits in a chair. I decide that is the noise I heard and Price agrees. Since we do not speak Yoruba and the watchman does not speak English, there is no way to tell him to move to the chair. So, I go to sleep listening to the steady noise of the creaky swing, liking its homey sound.

Friday, February 3rd

The heat gets worse. The sky has blue patches now instead of gray all over, but the heat is unreal. The sun is brighter, stronger than any place I have ever lived and not the slightest breeze. I could go crazy from the blazing sun. All I can think of is "when will this heat ever stop." I walk outside from our house to the classroom, always with a hat covering my head. The heat takes my breath. I can't easily walk but plod along, putting one foot after the other up the dirt path. I seem to be delivered over to heat waves blinding me from all sides. The glare and brightness hurts my head, my eyes.

Today I would trade my treasured pearl necklace for a sea breeze. Like the Englishwoman, Nan Fairbrother, "I want to wake up . . . with the sea-blink shining on the ceiling, like the light from snow but softer, and the day's business only to arrange when we shall swim because of the tide, the lovely uneven tide which banishes monotony in the most uneventful of holidays." I think longingly of July days and family reunions on a South Carolina beach, the feel of the surf and the morning air.

Inside the classroom this morning, the women sit listlessly with drawn, tired faces. One is asleep, her face down on her folded arms. I feel sick at my stomach, yet, somehow, I write words on the blackboard for these women to learn. Patience is holding Benjamin with her left arm and writing with her right hand. He wriggles and squirms and pulls at the gele on her head. She continues copying the words on her paper. She yearns to improve her English. At the end of this year, she will go with her husband John Akah, when he graduates, and with their seven children, to

45

help John minister to a church in Nigeria. Looking at her today, I wonder what the future will bring to her life.

Saturday, February 4th

Sitting by the window drinking coffee at 5:00 A.M., I do not light a candle. I am wondering about wisdom. Do I know who has it? Who doesn't? I ponder again that great line in Shakespeare's King Lear, when the fool shouts to the king, who is going mad, "Thou shouldst not have been old, till thou hadst been wise." Wisdom should come with age, but there is no guarantee that it will. I would choose to have wisdom over almost any other quality. A condensing of wisdom from all the experiences of one's life should be part of growing older. Along with the experiences of living, one has to keep storing the mind with good literature, music, and art, and REFLECT, REFLECT. All these things help provide wisdom. Yet I have known the uneducated man or woman who has garnered wisdom—good common sense along with knowing what really matters in life. I have been fortunate to spend my life with two educated, wise men. First, my dad and then my husband. So I know those persons who have wisdom when I am around them.

Sunday, February 5th

All the powdery dust is getting to me, I suppose. I woke up this morning with a hacking cough and a raw, tight throat. I know I am not feeling well. I go to church today because we are going to the big church in Ogbomosho. I want to see what goes on inside this enormous place.

Women sit on one side, men on the other. Children play in the dirt yard surrounding the church while services go on inside. Young people in the church create a steady rhythm with drums and *shakee-shakee*, a round gourd covered with a net, containing sewn-in cowrie shells. Announcements take fifteen minutes, each prayer is fifteen minutes long, and there are many prayers. Sitting here takes endurance. My throat hurts badly.

Riding back to the campus with the Gaventas, we close the car windows against the wind and dust outside. Even then, dust seems to assail my throat. We all go to Frances Jones for lunch. A lovely green cloth covers the table, with a green napkin by each place enfolding a small white lily. Matthew, the steward, did this flower arrangement. I am revived. Later, Martha gives me some green sulfa pills to take for my cough and infected throat. I don't know which will do me more good—Matthew's lilies or the green pills.

Monday, February 6th

Again today I stay in bed, coughing. Read and dozed during the morning. There was no electricity last night, thus no fan. I was miserable, sweating until the pillow under my head was wet. I could hear the night watchman's whistle. It made me remember a line by e. e. Cummings—something about "whistling far and wee." A comforting sound in the night. I need to have brought more cool, all cotton gowns for this climate. Anything made of polyester is too hot.

Price is helping finance an elderly woman trader. She borrows one *naira* ($1.60 US) each day and brings back produce for this loan of money. She speaks enough English to bargain well. One afternoon she had a lengthy conversation with Price on the back porch. I would guess the woman's age at over sixty. Price admires her willingness to work instead of begging, which would turn her into a non-person.

This afternoon Martha insists I go to her bedroom, the one air-conditioned room at Frances Jones. She wants me to rest and to listen to music on her new tape recorder. The green sulfa pills Martha prescribed for me are making me depressed, my usual reaction to sulfa. While I am in the room, Martha brings me a soft drink and ice cream. She has me keep my bare feet in a bucket of cold water to cool my body temperature. Such care and concern and, yet, she must have a line of women waiting at the hospital to see her.

Martha leaves and I glance around the plain, spare room. A bed, a chair, a dresser, a desk, and off the bedroom is a bathroom. Nothing fancy or luxurious here. Marjorie tells me Martha uses her money to help Nigerian people and never cares about what she has for herself. What a sense of freedom must be hers!

Tuesday, February 7th

Two miserable nights of heat, coughing, and a tightness in my chest. Not much sleep. I have not been to teach English class for two days.

Late yesterday afternoon the gnarled, little old man who waters all the potted plants and flowers on seminary campus knocked at our door. He heard I was sick and came to see how I was feeling. He resembles a little gnome. He said, "I asked Ba Ba (Price) about Ma Ma." Every day when I meet him on the campus, as I walk to English class, he tries to teach me a new word in the Yoruba language. So far I am learning only a few, like *tuo, okoro* and *ek'abo*. But he is always patient and cheerful. A good teacher and friend.

Coughing so long and deeply is agonizing. Strange how when one is sick the body gives up to the sickness for a time. Weariness settles in, the mind functions more slowly, nothing seems important but getting better. There is no book to read that could "take me lands away." All is grubby inside and outside. I lie in bed not wanting to talk. Price comes to the door with a glass of freshly-squeezed orange juice. I sip half the glass of juice to please him. After urging him to leave me and go eat his dinner at Frances Jones, I tell him not to bring me anything from there to eat. He thinks perhaps later I can try some toast and an egg. I make a faint reply and sink my head farther into the pillow.

Wednesday, February 8th

This morning my chest feels much better and coughing is minimal. The green pills worked wonders! I decide to teach the English class but cannot get much response from the women. The weather is still miserably hot and humid. Patience looks frazzled, and Benjamin grows heavier and heavier.

For lunch I fry together frozen potatoes that had turned a brownish black, onions, and chopped corn beef from a can. Hope the potatoes are OK. When I return to the States, what a shock awaits me to be again in a supermarket. I believe this sight would be enough to unnerve anyone coming from a Third World nation.

Rested three hours this afternoon and am going to teach the evening writing class. No electricity tonight. One of the students brings a lighted lantern to the classroom and we go on with our work. What would be a crisis at home is such a daily occurrence here that no one is excited or anxious.

When I return to our house, we have lights. I begin reading in the book of Amos in the Bible. Last week I agreed to write a daily devotional for the month of July, which will be used in a small devotional book, *Seek Daily*, prepared for students in Nigerian universities.

Thursday, February 9th

I lie awake thinking of our son, Philip, whose 24th birthday is today. Philip is our second son and third child. In his adolescent days, we measured his height on the frame of one kitchen door. He wanted badly to be 6 feet 3 inches, tall like his dad and brother. Finally, around age nineteen, he towered toward his goal. Along with his high intelligence, he has a caring, compassionate nature, an innate sweetness. I like the way he journeys, a believer in the good in people, adventuring and making the ordinary seem extraordinary. He is a day-brightener.

After class this morning, I go to the faculty lounge, drink cold water, and eat groundnuts. Talk among the faculty is about news from the States and who has any mail this day. Mail is the lifeline out here. No one can understand the importance of receiving a letter when this far away from home.

I walk home down the path past the pearly-white blossoms of the franjipani tree, seeing our clothes flapping on the line in the back yard. Nat has them washed and hung up by 8:00 A.M. Odd how soon a person can establish a routine anywhere in the world. Routine gives security to our lives, establishes order, and makes life more pleasant. The bad thing is never to vary it—to become a robot going about, not noticing, not adventuring, not caring. How does this happen to people? The Nigerians in this bush country live so simply, so much more in touch with the land and with people around them. I wonder if they, too, become creatures of routine. Somehow I doubt it because the unexpected happens here daily and the Africans live always with this uncertainty.

I go into our bedroom and see a lizard running fast as lightning across the floor, then under the bed where we sleep. I have never before seen one there. I chase it out, then it runs under the dresser and finally darts up the wall.

The glaring afternoon light is waning. I walk outside, nod to Moses, and inspect the vegetables in his garden. He stands at a distance, arms folded across his chest, with a questioning look on his face. I wonder about the age of Moses this day. I would like to shake his hand and tell him I am his friend.

I wish Price and I could be with Philip to help him celebrate his birthday. We sent a letter in a birthday card and hope it reaches him on this day. About all a parent can do when a child leaves the nest to be on his own, is to keep him close in love and prayer. Each child must find his or her own way. It would be so easy to be a smothering mother, yet one of the most difficult things in the world is to turn loose one's child into the world—like turning loose one's heart.

Friday, February 10th

Blue skies and white clouds this morning. We have only corn-flakes for breakfast, the one cereal that can be bought here. A few boxes are in the stores; they are sold to the foreigners living in Ogbomosho.

In the afternoon, Price and I go to an annual sports event on the seminary playing field. Another school comes here to compete in a soccer match with the seminary students. David, a brilliant student whom Price and I both teach, is goal keeper for the seminary team. He plays so intensely, diving and catching the ball, landing on his stomach on the dry hard ground. As the game ends, he is accidentally kicked in the neck by an opposing player.

Later, we pass him, sitting with another student on the steps of one of the seminary buildings. He looks ashy gray and cannot get his voice. Says he feels terrible. Price goes for our car. We take him and two other students to our house, get some ice to put in a cloth around his neck, and cold water for all of them to drink. When he begins to smile and feel better, we drive David and his friends back to their dorm.

David is such an intense person. He plays soccer like he does everything else, with all his might. He enters into discussion in class with great passion and vigor. He doesn't live life lightly. He interests me because he represents youth and enthusiasm and excitement. But he is already considered a hot head on campus. So his youthful spirit will gradually be squelched, and he will settle into a routine way of living. But if his high intelligence and fiery temperament could be channeled in the right direction, he could become quite a leader in this country. Too bad no one has the time over the years to see that he does this. I talk with him often, before and after writing class. It is not easy for him to drop his mask and talk freely and frankly because that is not the Nigerian way of relationship to the more educated person. I sense that he has bottled up his emotions, somewhat, and is sitting tight on them. All of which may lead to an explosive outburst someday, I'm afraid.

Saturday, February 11th

Price is coming to the house after his class this morning and going with me to shop for groceries in Ogbomosho. I have gone shopping with Alice or Enid since we arrived in January. Price wants to see what's inside these tin-roofed shacks and learn for himself the look of the town.

The morning is dusty and hot. Price and I drive to the center of town and park the car by an open stream of water, running in an open sewer along the side of the street. Black and white goats jump across the stream and continue going down the middle of the street. No street is paved and most have large unrepaired holes. From one store a radio blares loudly.

We go inside a grocery store where several people are asleep sitting upright on the floor. Two young people are dancing in the aisle to music from a radio. We wander by the shelves, waiting on ourselves. We end up with a box of cornflakes, four batteries for the torch, one bottle of orange drink, a bottle of bleach, a package of mints, two loaves of Nigerian-baked hard bread, and one can of chocolate drink.

We laugh together about this meager load of groceries compared to the numerous full bags we lug to the car in the States.

On another street women are selling tomatoes, red peppers, Nigerian bread, *efou* (Nigerian spinach), cassava, and yams. Cassava is a whitish tuber. After cooking it to a dough-like consistency called *geri*, Nigerians put a wad of this in their right hand and dip into other dishes of food to eat with the cassava. Women merchants, along this street, rest on upturned pans or buckets under the shade of trees, while a few sit in the glaring sunshine.

51

Other seats are small, low stools, which the women may occupy all day. Sometimes the women crouch in that peculiar African position, low to the ground, knees brought together, and hands clasped together, prayer-like. All the things to be sold are stacked haphazardly together.

What digs at my heart is the fact that these people may be doing the best they can, given the circumstances of their lives. Somehow there is an aliveness here amid all the disarray and noise, and the people themselves are clean.

Returning to the seminary entrance gate, we pass a mud house where a man sits on the front porch pedaling away at his sewing machine, making something of purple cloth. Men often do the tailoring and sewing.

Sunday, February 12th

I write today a description of the Frances Jones place, as I see it now, for remembrance in later days when I am far away from the familiar grassy-dirt driveway that circles the front of the house. Although I find it unbelievable that I will ever forget the evening walks there and back, or the house, or the people, I need to capture the details of that valued time when the clamor of the world was shut out for awhile, and where we sat leisurely around the dinner table relating to each other as person to person in a civilized and sensitive manner.

The house sits back from a dirt road with a half-circle drive in front. Between the drive in front of the house and the dirt road is a large grassy area. Tall palm trees, flame trees, and frangipani grow there. Around the screened-in porch in front of the house Martha planted flower bulbs and other blooming perennial plants so that always colorful flowers appear, like roses or lilies. On the porch, overlooking the grass and trees are a wooden swing—the old-fashioned kind hung by two chains from the ceiling—and several large rocking chairs. The first room inside is the living room, which opens into the dining room. The long dining table is usually covered with a white tablecloth, topped with a center-piece of fresh flowers, arranged by Matthew.

In the late afternoon, 5:30 P.M. or so, we walk from our house up a dirt and grass-covered lane, and turn into the dirt road that leads to the half-circle drive.

Marjorie plans the meals, and Sam cooks them. She travels to Ibadan once a month, to bring back a supply of food. Sam goes to market in Ogbomosho for tomatoes, peppers, eggs, and other local produce. Once a month a trader from Ibadan comes, carrying a sack of potatoes, or carrots, or onions, which he sells door to door.

Matthew stands at the corner of the dining table, keeping the dishes on a tea trolley, or goes to the kitchen for refills. When we finish eating, he clears the table of food and dishes, then serves a dessert—usually fresh fruit or canned fruit with banana.

Later, most of us go to sit in the living room or on the porch, if the evening is not too sultry, and talk with Marjorie and Martha or guests at the house.

Soon the tropical night sky is aglow with stars—so many no one can look without exclaiming in wonderment. Reluctantly, Price and I say "good night" and, by the light of our torch, walk to our house.

Monday, February 13th

Up for a dawn breakfast by candlelight. For the cornflakes we use powdered milk mixed with water. In our refrigerator, milk remains cold as long as the electricity works. When it doesn't, we use warm milk and wait for the power to return.

Price and I go this morning to visit Ruth Womack's Kersey Home, three miles from the town. Ruth has been in Nigeria for more than thirty years, caring for malnourished mothers and their babies who come from the bush country. Mothers, carrying their babies, walk miles to the Kersey Home where they will live until both mother and baby are well. News of the house spreads by word of mouth in the bush area. Ruth gives the mothers milk to drink, boiled eggs, and fruit. Mothers and babies sleep on mats on the concrete floors of the house. The women appear emaciated, some practically skin and bones, the babies the same, some covered with boils, their hair in thin wisps.

Sanitation at the house is a problem because water has to be carried from a distant stream. The odor of unwashed bodies is strong in the heat of this noon day. Ruth cradles a sickly baby in her arms, patting his small bottom. She says he was near death when he and his mother arrived a week ago. Now he is gaining weight on the bottled milk. She loves them all.

I am so overcome by the sights and smells that I go outside for air. A girl of ten or twelve years, beautiful of face, walks toward the house, carrying a bucket of water on her head. Nearing me, she smiles sweetly. I return the smile. She passes on into the house and I stand there, my head hanging, weeping quietly. Price comes outside, gray color in his face, and with troubled eyes.

I am at a loss for words.

Price breaks the silence. "Ruth is a saint, isn't she?" His speaking is like he is talking to himself. "Compared to what we do—teaching—Ruth's and Hazel's work is the most self-giving and emotionally difficult work done here."

"I think one of the greatest sins may be not to be a saint," I muse.

We get into Ruth's car for the drive returning to Ogbomosho. Price and I are visibly shaken. Ruth admonishes, "Don't despair. So many are being saved and many more will be."

Ruth and Hazel are Mother Theresas in Nigeria; their lives are a glory.

Tuesday, February 14th

We slept later this morning, rising at 7:00 A.M. Gloria comes to clean the house today. She is a tiny, young-looking woman. Her husband, also named David, is in his last year of study at the seminary. When they leave here, Gloria and David will return to Ibo country, where their roots are, to be with their families and tribe. Gloria moves quickly about the house, sweeping and cleaning, and doesn't talk unless I talk to her. She has a good command of English.

However, this morning she tells Price and me the story of the death of one of her children, an eight-year-old boy. She believes her husband's brother, a witch doctor, put a curse on the child. This brother was angry because David left the tribe to become a Christian. Gloria said the witch doctor told them that this curse would affect the child's back. Her eyes widen and her voice gets louder and more excited as she tells how, later, this child suddenly became ill, with great pain in his back, and was taken to the Baptist Hospital here. The doctors could find no reason for his pain. His illness ended in death. Yet she and her husband will return to where such tribal beliefs still exist. I tell her she has a strong faith and is very brave.

I wish for a movie camera and a tape recorder as Gloria talks. She is more dramatic and intense than any actress in a tragic role. Except this was a real tragedy for Gloria.

Clouds appear in the sky late today. The sunshine is not as harsh and bright as usual. I am going to survive this heat. I walk to the hospital for a blood test Martha wants me to have, due to the infectious cough. "Your blood count is super," she reports.

When Price comes from his office, he brings me pink blossoms from the frangipani tree as a Valentine gift. I had forgotten that it was Valentine's Day! How lovely for Price to remember!

Wednesday, February 15th

This evening we go to the Richardson's house to talk to three Fulani, members of a nomadic tribe who wander with their cattle from Senegal to the Sudan across Africa. They may have originated from the Senegal River Valley. Some Muslims, illiterates as well as literates, and influential administrators migrated to what is now north of Nigeria in the eleventh century, mainly as nomadic cattle herders. Cattle are their wealth; they are not even slaughtered except at times of births or weddings. The Fulani live in open grazing country, quickly constructing a temporary hut of straw. They are small in stature, the women fine-boned with slender bodies and regal bearing.

J. W. Richardson, an older, tall, slim man, has been a missionary among these people for many years. Tonight a missionary from the Cameroon has come to do the translation of the Fulani (Nigritic) language for us. Five of the national languages spoken in Nigeria are English, Hausa, Fulani, Yoruba, and Igbo.

The three Fulani men tell us about marriage customs among their people. Elaborate negotiations must take place before a Fulani man gets a bride. His older brother must go to the bride's uncle, older brother of the father, and seek permission for the girl to be given in marriage. This ceremonial rite goes on for as little as two weeks but more often lasts months or years, with at least seven such visits being made. The father wants to know the extent of the groom's wealth. The groom sends gifts of cowrie shells and kola nuts.

After finally consenting, the bride's father invites guests for a big feast. A Muslim ceremony, with reading from the Koran, may be held without the bride or groom present. Afterwards, the groom goes to get the bride and they will leave to live apart from the Fulani group for a while. The father may change his mind at any time during the negotiations. The older brother keeps the groom's cattle while the groom is away, and earlier the groom-to-be keeps the older brother's cattle while the older brother sees about his future wife.

Such complex rituals these seem, compared to our Western-style courtship and marriage. The families on both sides are deeply involved in the courtship, as well as the prospective marriage. Maybe it would be a better arrangement in our culture if parents could provide input into the selecting of a mate for their children, rather than leaving the matter to chance or luck, as we seem to do.

Thursday, February 16th

I write this while I remember. So soon these brilliant colors in the clothes men and women wear at ceremonial occasions will fade from my mind when I return to the States. I want to list them because they are as gorgeous as the fully-spread tail of a peacock. Men wear pink, coral, purple, lavender, cream, green, pale orange, bright orange, apricot lace, copper-colored hats embroidered in gold, cut lace in raspberry red and silver, eyelet material in hot pink, or all white. Yellow eyelet worn with a red fez; kelly green, royal blue, aqua and silver worn with a white fez; pale green, yellow, turquoise, and fez of gold; and pink and green, coral, peacock blue lace, with an aqua and magenta fez or a silver and blue fez.

The village chiefs wear long, double strands of coral beads. In church, women wear the *gele* (pronounced "gaily"), an intricately-wrapped head turban, in pale gray taffeta, embroidered in gold, royal blue, deep orange or wine red and gold. Other turbans are turquoise, gold, green, blue or pink. For church some women may wear five or six gold bracelets, long earrings, necklaces of gold; these are usually the women traders, who put their money into gold jewelry. These dressed-up women have a proud bearing, a pride of identity. Surely the headdress outdoes any chapeau found in a shop of the Champs Elysees!

I cook a canned chicken this afternoon. Looks as small as a quail. Price could eat it in four bites, I believe. The outside of the can reads, "Canned in Des Moines, Iowa." What a long way from there to a store in Ibadan where Enid bought it for us. The meat was as tough and tasteless as a Nigerian chicken.

Friday, February 17th

Every day brings an opportunity to help someone. Small things, but needed. I give tangerines and oranges to the night watchman and to Moses—some extra pay—and food to Gloria. Today I'm taking a boiled egg, an orange, and some candy to Rebecca, one of my students in English class. Yesterday she went to the hospital for the birth of her child, ten minutes after she was in class. Thomas, in the writing class, loves books and I brought him a book from Ibadan. The book contains stories and poems by a Nigerian writer, Chinua Achebe. Achebe published novels in the 1950s which were acclaimed at home and abroad. His first two novels, *Things Fall Apart* and *No Longer at Ease*, dealt powerfully with the problems of living in a rapidly changing society. Later he wrote *Arrow of God*, *A Man of the People*, and a collection of poetry, *Beware Soul Brother*.

For Patience I buy buttons for her to sew on clothes worn by her seven boys. I decide to do without soft drinks while here and give the money instead to Ruth Womack to buy milk for the babies she tends. Before we go home I intend to give most of my clothes to women my size in the English class.

This is the way people should live, helping others in tangible ways, not giving money only. To look into someone's face when handing that person food or a gift brings a joy all its own. We, of the upper and the middle classes of America, are too isolated from the poor. Volunteer work is not always the answer. This can rob the poor of their dignity by being too patronizing. Here, living among and being with those who need help allows you to give of yourself as well as to give something to that person. That way you are brothers and sisters together as God meant us to be.

We are up at dawn. No electricity and no fan going most of the night. Too hot to sleep. Dawn is the coolest time now. So we eat dawn breakfasts by the open window—a light and airy time.

Last night Price and I were invited for the first time to a meal in a Nigerian home—that of the superintendent of the hospital. Alice and Bill were guests also. This Nigerian's house was a modern concrete-block painted house, not mud. We sat in the living room with the superintendent and his wife, when we arrived. A large TV was blaring loudly. No one turned it off, and we had to talk above the noise. On one table was a red candle, hymn books were piled high on a piano, and straight chairs and several benches provided seating places. Scattered about the room on tables and on the wall were at least forty framed pictures of family. Nine people—the extended family—live here. A few of the superintendent's brother's children are in this extended family, as are grandparents.

The superintendent made a formal welcoming speech to us, then said a prayer. We walked to a dining room and served ourselves, buffet-style. Each dish had a top to cover it. There were white china plates and stainless steel forks and knives. The superintendent wore dressy flowered pants and tunic, and a soft purple turban hat that looked as though it had been twisted and smashed to the side. His wife wore a long, pink skirt and blouse and pink gele on her head, with a bow tied in back. One man, a cosmetics salesman from the capital city, Lagos, sat down, took off one of his shoes and massaged his foot and toes. He wasn't embarrassed. Before we went for our food, the superintendent's wife curtsied to us and bowed on one knee to Bill Gaventa, for whom she works at the hospital.

The food was rice, fried chicken (tough and scrawny) in hot pepper sauce, *fufu* (pounded yam) with melon soup, *efou* (spinach cooked in melon oil with onion), little cakes of mashed black-eyed peas, *akara* (fried bean bread), then fried plantain with hot sauce (this was heavy with palm oil), ice water, and banana cake that Alice brought. Surprisingly, the small bite of *efou* that I tasted was good but looked, as always, slimy and green. The heavy, unfamiliar taste of palm oil was difficult to swallow and saturated the flavor of everything. I ate a very small amount. We sat in chairs and held our plates in our laps.

Normally, most Nigerians do not sit down together at the table and eat meals. Food is cooked, put in covered dishes and left on a table. Men eat first, then women and children. The superintendent's seventy-year-old mother cooked most of this meal outside, in pots over a wood fire, we were told.

When we left, Alice said to the hosts, *"Ek'aro, ekunowo,"* which I think translates from Yoruba to mean, "Well done, I salute you for spending money." Their way of saying, "Thanks for having us, you went to so much trouble."

Sunday, February 19th

Hooray! We have freshly-squeezed orange juice for breakfast. And a large glass at that. Last night Price used sixteen small oranges, from the trees in the orchard, to get enough for two glassfuls. I had almost forgotten how delicious fresh juice tastes.

Today is a Muslim national holiday. Such religious holidays are observed by the Muslims with the slaughtering of goats. The greatest concentration of believers are in northern Nigeria. Virtually all the Muslims in Africa are Sunni. Also in a number of places are missionaries of the unorthodox Ahmaddiyya sect (with headquarters in Pakistan), whose influence is perhaps greater than their number. This sect has pioneered in translating the Koran into African vernaculars.

Other than Roman Catholic, Protestant, and Muslim believers in this country, there are other groups sometimes termed independents and separatists. Often established by leaders who split from mission-founded churches, one group of these churches is called Aladura churches. The term, meaning "one who prays," indicates their particular emphasis on prayer for physical and spiritual healing. Worship is vigorous and exuberant, making use of African musical instruments, dancing, drumming, and processions. High value is placed on the harmony and unity of the fellowship and on the individual within himself.

It seems to me that the human person, wherever he is, pursues holiness in some form and longs for wholeness. Religion has a great hold on people living in this continent.

Monday, February 20th

Slept well last night, one of the few times since being here I have slept soundly through the night. We are near the main highway South to Lagos, North to Ilorin. Everything transported into this country is hauled by big trucks going night and day up and down this road. By early morning the droning noise of truck tires can be heard on the road. I like to be awake before I can hear traffic and to be a part of the awakening time for animals, plants, and earth.

After English class I took snapshots with my camera of the women. They were funny. Each one wanted to be in the front line. I had difficulty getting them to stand still. They were noisy, pushy, and chattering. The scene reminded me of an old-time, silent film comedy. They kept saying they were not dressed "fine, fine." I told them I would take another picture when they could all dress up in their fine, fine. I like all of these women, each one so different in looks and personality and intelligence. What a privilege it is to get to know them, to commune face to face with our feelings, even with their broken English. So here in the bush, in up-country Africa we are persons alike, each with God-given distinctiveness.

Martha says more and more patients in the hospital here are coming in with hepatitis, malaria, and tuberculosis. Price and I are faithfully taking preventive malaria tablets daily and drinking only filtered water. I hope we stay well.

Tuesday, February 21st

Joy, joy! We go on a picnic tonight to the Ogbomosho reservoir—all of us who eat at Frances Jones. Martha and Marjorie engineer the affair. Sam and Matthew prepare baskets of food at the house. We have potato salad, fried chicken, spaghetti with onion and tomato sauce, egg salad, new carrots, pineapple, raisin salad, and cake, along with a local orange fruit drink that is thirst-quenching but tasteless. The road to the reservoir is rough and full of deep holes all the way. From the car we carry folding chairs to the top of the dam at the water's edge. This reservoir was built a few years ago by a team of engineers from Israel.

Oh, how great to see water and large patches of green grass surrounding the lake, or reservoir. And to think this area was once a somewhat hollow plain where elephants roamed. In the lush, green land far off we can see small fires burning, where people live. We sit in our chairs, watching an orange-red sun ride low in the sky and disappear, followed later by a pale gold, full moon rising overhead. All of us feel the magic of our time together in this quiet, cool place by the water. We stop talking and sit quietly, absorbing the delightful mystery and beauty of the evening. An unforgettable freshness compensates for some of the heat and daily routine of work.

Three months from today we will be leaving Nigeria. Already I know I will carry this land and its people in my heart forever. As Doris Lessing wrote: "That (Africa) is not a place to visit unless one chooses to be an exile ever afterwards from an inexplicable majestic silence lying just over the border of memory or of thought. Africa gives you the knowledge that man is a small creature, among other creatures, in a large landscape."

Wednesday, February 22nd

Up at daylight, grade some papers, look over what I will teach in English class today. I am having the women read aloud once a week from their book of stories with simple English sentences. This means we must stop and work on pronunciation, the meaning of words, and how the use of the word is similar or different from the word in their languages.

While the women practice reading silently before they read aloud, I take Benjamin from Patience and put him in the baby crib in the corner. I wiggle a stuffed toy in front of his face until he falls asleep. Then I hold Catherine's tiny daughter, Joy. I walk to the door in the classroom and along the narrow outside corridor. She lays her head on my shoulder and sleeps.

Thursday, February 23rd

A hot and humid night kept me turning and tossing, and the air is heavy with heat now at 6:00 A.M.

I walk to the window wishing I could feel a light and lovely breeze, fern-fresh like one feels on an early summer morning in the mountains. No breeze at all, only windless air, and the teak leaves are falling, falling like the sound of time. Rilke says so beautifully:

The leaves are falling, falling as from far up,
as if orchards were dying high in space.
Each leaf falls as if it were motioning "no."
And tonight the heavy earth is falling
away from all the other stars in the loneliness.
We're all falling. This hand here is falling.
And look at the other one . . . . It's in them all.
And yet there is Someone, whose hands
infinitely calm, hold up all this falling.

I commit these days to memory to bring them out someday like reading old, faded letters. I am learning the secret of *being* rather than constantly *doing*. I like the serenity this provides.

Friday, February 24th

Last night was hot and humid, even though we slept with two fans stirring. Price needs a haircut, but there is no barber here. Last night we walked to the Whirley's house for Carl to trim Price's hair. Carl is the man for all seasons. He is a plumber, electrician, barber, and mechanic for the seminary. Both Carl and Enid are modest about their abilities, very different from some presidents of colleges and seminaries.

Today we are going with Mofeku, driving to Ibadan. How I dread going on the highway again. Drivers with no licenses drive 80 or 90 miles per hour. No highway patrol anywhere, and no one cares how fast you drive. There are horrible wrecks of lorries, trucks, and private cars daily.

We are going to stay overnight in Ibadan with the Edgar Burks, who work at the Baptist mission there. When we leave Ogbomosho, all the car windows are open to get air; I have to wear a scarf over my head to keep wind from blowing and tangling my hair. I feel smothered by the furnace-like hot air and the clinging scarf. We begin to pass small villages with their shacks and mud houses. Lorries speed around us, loaded with people. Baskets and bundles protrude from windows and are tied to the top of each lorry. We are on a two-lane highway. Twice Mofeku pulls the car to the shoulder of the road, in order to avoid an oncoming lorry passing a car on a hill. My stomach tightens into a knot.

After two hours' driving, we reach the Burks' house, a lovely, old mud and concrete home. Trees and blooming flowers and grass all behind a gate and fences. Inside the house are high ceilings, large windows back and front, and spacious, cool rooms. Edgar and Linnie Jane, his wife, walk with us to the back yard where purple and white orchids bloom on trunks of tall palm trees.

Edgar wants to know what we think of Nigeria. Price answers that he is having a rich and rewarding experience overall. He thinks the students at the seminary are highly motivated and a joy to teach. He especially likes their enthusiasm.

I agree with all Price reports, but add, "I wish the roads weren't so dangerous to travel. I'm scared to death every time we start on a trip. Price wants to see as much of this country as possible before we leave, but I'm not sure I can do that."

The Burks invite me to come and stay with them, if I decide not to go east to Eku or Benin City with Price later on. I'm grateful for their care but know I'll probably go adventuring with my husband, in spite of my apprehensions. Price says we might go to Kano when we travel up north in Nigeria. Kano is where camel caravans stopped long ago on their way to Timbuktu.

Once in bed I go to sleep watching waving palm fronds outside the window, silhouetted against the light from a full moon. The pleasant ambience of this house, and being with friends, brings a welcome emotional refreshment.

Saturday, February 25th

Cannot believe I tossed and turned in bed all night after such a peaceful evening with friends.

We leave with the Burks for a long morning of seeing sights in Ibadan, which rambles across a series of low hills, a dense sea of corrugated tin roofs in the midst of a few modern blocks. We go to the Dominican Monastery where batik cloth shirts are made by the Nigerian employees of the monastery.

From there we visit the University of Ibadan, a sprawling campus, cream-colored buildings, its own zoo. The university has a medical school, hospital, and archaeological museum. Students tuition and room and board are paid by the government.

We return to the Burks' house for lunch and a rest, away from the heat and humidity. My energy level is zero. Price looks wilted. It is hotter in Ibadan than in Ogbomosho and more traffic.

People clog the streets and sidewalks wherever we drive in the downtown sections. We can only inch along in the car or when walking. Going so slowly we do have a chance to see the goods being sold along the sidewalks. Red pepper, shoes, tomatoes, and cloth. Photo, mechanic shops, hair dressing places, and medical labs.

Once I exclaim, "Look at that!" in disbelief. A woman is doing her family wash at a spigot in the midst of the flow of people. We spot a cola drink sign, the only familiar sight in this throng of people. As if the gates to a sports arena had opened to let out the fans, the mass of bodies fill the streets.

There is a water shortage in the city and men, women, and children huddle around water spigots to collect water in buckets. Garbage in gross-looking piles litters the corner intersections and overflows on the sidewalk. On one corner where we stop for traffic, a woman under a tin roof in a dirt-floored hut is cooking yams and wrapping them in teak leaves to sell to passers-by.

All I can say as we drive along the streets is "Oh my, oh my."

Sunday, February 26th

I am relieved when we turn in under the arch that marks the beginning of the seminary campus. Missionary people entering there after a trip always exclaim, "Thank you, Lord." That is my prayer too.

This afternoon I work on writing a story about my impression of Ibadan. It is difficult to describe the reality of that place and the emotions I felt.

Monday, February 27th

This morning school boys descended on the guava trees in the back of the house and stripped them of all the guavas. Moses was in the garden at the time and did not stop them. Perhaps he was afraid. They outnumbered him by four to one.

I am saving buttons and trying to find some in the small cloth shops. Mothers sew most clothes for their children, and zippers are both expensive and difficult to find. A small bag of buttons here is $1.80 (US).

These married students do not have to pay tuition or for their living quarters. They do have to pay for all other expenses. Some students get loans from the school or help from their families. I do not know how the students provide for so many children! I think they must be good managers.

Tuesday, February 28th

What a joy it is to have time for contemplation. Pure joy. Here where so many of life's non-essentials are eliminated, the self centers on the essential, quiets down, listens, observes, and feels more in harmony with God's world. We do not need for living all that we think we need. What is most important is to know what we are living for and then to live as if each day is a gift from God. I have thought this before but can put the belief into better practice here. Simone Weil was right when she believed that everything which was of value in her came from outside herself, not as a gift but as a loan which must be renewed again and again.

We have allowed television, newspapers, and telephones to so intrude upon our lives that we are all but slaves to them. They take over our lives demonically and we end up making habit of their use. We are no longer free. Surely the day will never come when every thatched hut in the village compounds will support a television antenna. Horrors!

My time of sitting by the window goes too quickly this morning. I blow out the flame on the candle, try the light switch, and have lights.

"Aren't you feeling well," Price wants to know this morning.

"If I have a gloomy face, it's because I'm pining for a letter from Doug, Sara, or Philip," I am quick to answer.

"I know, I'd like to hear, too," and adds, thinking aloud, "Doug is busy with university teaching, Sara looking after her two little boys, and Philip busy with working in North Carolina." Price is trying to console me.

He thinks they have written and the mail is being held up somewhere along the way. He says he knows they have written before now, and I do too. "We'll surely hear this week," he predicts, "If we don't, I'll write you a letter!"

MARCH

Wednesday, March 1

A glorious morning! We receive letters from two of our children. All is well with them. Both have written letters which we have not received. Yes, the mail system here is unreliable.

On the way to Ibadan a few days ago, I was tense because of the highway conditions. I was fretting inside, too, over not hearing from our children. I looked out the window toward the aqua blue sky and prayed quietly for their welfare. Suddenly I felt an overwhelming closeness to God, and the world dissolved momentarily while a voice spoke to my inner consciousness. Clearly I felt I was being told to leave my doubts and worries and to trust God. God's grace and love seemed to flow through me as I had never before experienced in my life. I told no one of this and am writing it down in order to have a record.

How difficult it is to talk or write about personal spiritual experiences without sounding glib or too righteous. To read the lives of women saints like Theresa of Avila or Catherine of Siena is to learn of how much time they devoted to quiet and prayer and contemplation. Saint Theresa said, "Do not be deceived by anyone. Prayer is the only way that leads to the Fountain. You must of necessity practice mental prayer and even attain to contemplation, if God grants you the grace." Perhaps only the saints can express mystical illumination.

I walk to the hospital this afternoon to talk to a student wife in the maternity ward. The hospital is a depressing place because of the conditions there, so unlike hospitals in the States. Due to water shortages, women lie on mattresses without sheets and pillows without pillowcases. The smell of urine and blood loads the air. Stretchers in the hallway are bloodstained. Floors look dirty. Hospital staff and attendants do the best they can under difficult circumstances. We are told the government-run hospitals are in worse condition. The mission doctors in this Baptist hospital in Ogbomosho are caring, patient, and hard-working. Even under these conditions mothers and infants are saved from a death that occurs frequently in the more primitive bush country without any medical care.

Thursday, March 2nd

Nat here to wash clothes at 7:00 A.M. Filling tubs, and washing, and rinsing by the water spigot at the rear of the house, he will have the clothes hung on the line in an hour's time. Moses is raking leaves that have fallen among the shrubbery by the windows and is sweeping the front and back porches. He comes to the back door with a small tangerine and a guava in his hands. He always brings the ripe fruit from the trees to me, which I share with him. The first time I gave him back an orange, I don't think he understood my meaning. I smiled, pointed to the orange in his hand, pointed to him, and nodded my head. He walked away with the orange, looking puzzled, but after that he would accept what I gave him.

The sky is shadowed with raggedy clouds—no sunshine—a pleasant change, with soft wisps of breeze blowing at the window.

I do not mind being alone in this house, or in any place, and am thankful I can enjoy solitude. Solitude can be a time for contemplation or for pure joy, or mind struggling. Solitude affords many moods. In my own home, I have a piercing sense of being alive when, alone, I listen to Spanish guitar music while arranging phlox and lilies, hand-picked from our flower garden. Or I wait, sitting quietly, not apathetically, but fighting inwardly to discipline myself to manage in a better way a problem I've created or encountered. In the nineteenth century Emily Herman, wife of a Presbyterian minister, said, "It takes courage amid the charitable bustle of the day to seek the soul's sanctuary, and remain in stillness before its utmost shrine until we know what God means us to be, and therefore what he means us to do." I agree!

Friday, March 3rd

After breakfast I take my coffee and sit at the window looking out toward Moses' garden. My thoughts return again and again to our older son, Douglas, far away in Wisconsin. He is an archaeologist and a professor at the University of Wisconsin in Madison. He toils long hours at his career and could qualify as a mild workaholic, I suppose. His work has brought him significant recognition in teaching, numerous financial grants, and esteem from colleagues in his field of study. The fact that he maintains his integrity and kindness warms my pride in him. Yes, he has purity of heart. I hope he takes time along the way to smell the flowers.

I hold my children close to my heart's core in prayer. In this place, I am learning prayer is not something I come to at certain times of the day or evening, but that I live and move and have my being in constant prayer. This has been a beautiful and comforting discovery. I am always only moments away from prayer in petition, in gratitude, in joy, in depression, in fear. These conversations with God give meaning to the inner life I yearn earnestly to pursue. Would I have ever found this way had we not come to Africa? Who's to say? I am not a fatalist. I do believe, however, that those things which happen in our lives are only those things which can happen in God's providence.

Saturday, March 4th

How expressive are some of the Nigerian sayings. I have learned a few of them. If someone goes to a house to visit and no one is home, the person visiting will say to the absent person the next time they meet, "I came and met your absence," or "I met the broken dish." How much more imaginative than our western equivalent, "Sorry you weren't at home." Another is a Hausa saying to a person leaving on a journey, "May you come down in peace" or "May you arrive in peace."

Gloria is here to clean the house. She goes from room to room, singing in a low-key, non-disturbing way. It is as though she sings to herself some words in her tribal tongue. The sound carries overtones of elemental things.

Tonight Alice comes to take Price and me to Ogbomosho's night market. Women traders are everywhere, spreading their wares in front of them as they sit on the ground—baskets of hot red peppers, bracelets of ground glass, old Portuguese trading beads, and hand-woven cloth used to tie babies around the mother's back in a carrying position. The market area is unlighted except for here and there the glow from odd-looking kerosene lamps, made of small milk cans. Several women fry cassava patties in palm oil on a tin top covering a low fire. Price buys and eats one of the patties. Nigerians standing around watch as he eats, then cheer and raise their arms with a clinched fist, which here means, "I like you, good work." Later, Price gives a beggar woman, wearing gold earrings, some money, and she raises her arm with a clinched fist!

In the darkness of the night, with the little lamps and the black faces vying to outshine each other in anticipation of a purchase from our passing by, I am giddy with excitement over what we might see next. Suddenly we walk in front of a table spread with an eerie assortment of small and large bones, dead bird feathers, seeds, weird and dark dried masses. A wizened Nigerian man, with only a scrap of hair on top of his head, sits on a stool behind the table. He is a tribal medicine man, selling his treatments for all illnesses.

Sunday, March 5th

A hot night! I did not sleep soundly and am up at 6:00 A.M to make coffee. We buy coffee in small tin cans from Kenya. It is stronger and more mellow than the same brand we buy in the States. Early in the morning and the air is heavy and still.

After arriving here, we were loaned an Opel car to drive, one of many provided mission personnel. The car did not give Price enough leg room, and Carl exchanged it for an Audi. We drive it only on the seminary compound or for groceries or to church. Today we drive up the highway to Antioch Baptist Church, across the road from the hospital. Outside the hospital, people are crowded together waiting to get inside. Some will wait the long day before it's their turn to see a doctor.

Marjorie teaches the Sunday School class I attend. She loves the women in this class, the student wives that she teaches housewifery (a British term) during the week. She has the ability to be firm yet warm and giving toward them. Marjorie sets high

72

standards for herself and expects the women to discipline themselves.

We meet in a small corner room at the rear of the church. One window and a door are kept open in the room, bare of furnishings except for uncomfortable hardwood chairs.

Tonight we return to the church to hear students from Bendel State in Nigeria sing songs in their native language, with only the beating of drums to accompany them. All are dressed in long skirts of orange, pink, red, and purple, strewn with flower, animal, bird, or tree designs. Men wear the long skirts with shirts, and women, skirts with blouses to match. The students clap their hands and sway with the drum beat while they sing. I, too, feel the joy they express with their singing and with their body movements.

Later, a gusty rain suddenly descends as we drive toward our place. Wonderful to smell the rain. I rush in the house to pull down windows but hate to shut out the breeze which so revives me. The rain pounds the hard, dry earth. This should settle the dust and provide water for the town's reservoir. A really tropical rainstorm delighting ears and nose and eyes. I suddenly realize I have never felt this grateful for rain before.

Monday, March 6th

I meet a student named David this morning, in my office at the seminary, to talk with him about the editorial he is writing for the "Theologue" magazine (one the students publish). His dark eyes flash and shine as he talks excitedly about what he believes. He has so much enthusiasm; it is hardly containable within his mind and body. His words dance and accelerate the longer he talks. Today he is concerned that there is not more interaction between the students and the faculty. He thinks there should be more fellowship, more of a sense of community between these two groups. Some of his ideas are sound and others lack the maturity of judgment he has yet to achieve. I listen and try to guide him toward a more reasonable way of stating his beliefs. Reading all the material written for the magazine has meant eight hours of extra work, but there was need for some careful editing.

Price and I are to be speakers in chapel on Thursday. I do not like to do any public speaking. I ask him to help me work on something we can present together. We decide to do a dialogue on martyrdom. In it, he and I will talk about some of history's martyrs and what martyrdom means. We will use passages from T. S. Eliot's *Murder in the Cathedral.* My favorite lines from that play are those spoken by Archbishop Thomas Becket, trying to comfort the chorus of women when King Henry's knights come to kill him. Becket says, "Human kind cannot bear very much reality."

Rain last night left the earth underneath soft and mushy, quite a change from the aridity all last month. I broke off some deep-colored, rose-red blossoms from the frangipani tree to bring in the house. They remind me of springtime. I can find no vase in the house, but the blossoms look lovely enough in a drinking glass.

Tonight we attend a baby-naming ceremony for the Oyedepo's newborn baby girl. Every newborn baby at the seminary has a naming ceremony given by the parents. The program is a formal one, with a chairman, who has the opening speech, then scripture reading, prayer, naming of the baby, and dedication. Then comes a social time with refreshments of orange drink and hard candy. Some person skilled in telling jokes and riddles comes forward to entertain the invited guests. A special chorus of selected students sings. The chairman, usually a professor, makes the closing speech.

When we return to our house, I realize I have forgotten the baby's name in the midst of all that was taking place!

Tuesday, March 7th

Students here are very imaginative. Their minds do not have a sophisticated veneer. One student, daily, does all the flower arrangements for the chapel. They paint posters to display on bulletin boards, act in plays, sing, play drums, and arrange their own entertainment.

As I walk home from English class I notice green spots on the sere brown grass. The mango tree looks more shiny and new. Could it be possible things are greening? The sky is losing its hard, steel-gray color for a softer, smoky, pale one. I gaze upward longing for some sign of blue or puffy white clouds. There is a strangeness to the sky, thus far, that is unusual when the sun shines.

Darkness comes quickly now, 5:00 P.M. and total blackness envelopes the land.

I had forgotten what a night is like without artificial lights. I relish the dark nights, the quietness. And oh the stars! So often I forget to look at the stars at home. Here I cannot forget! In Africa you cannot forget anything. Here many thousands upon thousands of stars twinkle brightly, close together, crowding the heavens. Looking up is like viewing a black velvet cloth studded with diamonds stretched over my head. Often, we can only stand in silence looking in awe under the stars. To talk would be too much.

Paul and Eveline Miller, who teach here, come to see us tonight to talk about our trip to Yankari Game Reserve in northern Nigeria. Paul will drive their car. It will be a long, difficult journey, but we will see a very different region of Nigeria. We will climb by car to more mountainous country and to a cooler climate, stopping at Jos overnight both going and coming. I am excited over going but dread being on the highways again. No matter, if we are to see any of these places while here, we must travel by car, since there is no easy way to travel by train or plane.

Eveline was a student in Price's class at Furman University when she was on furlough. She wanted Price to come teach students in Ogbomosho. We will make the trip from Ogbomosho to Kaduna with the Whirleys, then we will leave with the Millers from Kaduna for Jos. The Millers are taking their youngest daughter to the school in Jos for missionary children.

Paul says we will like Jos, where the humidity is lower and the town is cleaner. He warns that the ride to the game reserve, called Yankari, will be long and through dry, dusty land, at a lower elevation. I wince and look toward Price.

"Are you sure you want to go, Leslie?" Price queries.

"Oh, I'm game for it, if you are," I answer back quickly, assuming an air of bravado.

Secretly, I welcome this foray into the unknown, providing more substance for the soul and spirit than routine existence. We will have to take our own drinking water and food, Eveline reminds us. We can ride in a truck in the game reserve seeing the animals. If we are lucky, we might see elephants, Paul reports.

"What else?" I want to know.

"Wildebeest, baboons, water buffalo, hartebeest, and tropical birds," Paul answers.

"Any lions?" I ask.

"Not likely," he says.

I am disappointed, for of all animals I would like to see in the wild are the lions. I have always felt sympathy for the caged lions in zoos, pacing or sleeping, bereft of their natural habitat.

Wednesday, March 8th

When we awake at 6:00 A.M., there is no electricity. I reach for the torch on the bedside table and make my way to the kitchen. I walk to the back door, look out into the darkness and see a tiny woman gathering up the teakwood leaves into a bundle. How long has she been there?

A pearl-colored light widens the sky while I watch this skinny little woman tie up her bundle of leaves, throw it over her back, and trudge down the road. I long to talk to her and to know more about her. But between her life and my life there is a gulf as wide as the ocean I have crossed to reach this place. So, too, each of us dwell in our own country of mind and heart, worlds apart. Did she ever dream or yearn for a better life, or is surviving her only thought? Sad that I will never know.

Our morning talk on martyrdom goes well enough. The students are attentive. My voice is not strong enough for public speaking. I doubt if anyone sitting in the back of the chapel could hear me because there was no amplification. Oh, well, I am glad that is over. My thoughts have been on the leaf-gathering woman this day.

Thursday, March 9th

I am in low spirits this morning. I miss being able to talk on the phone with our children. Letters from them are great, but I need to hear their voices.

Moses is digging in the garden back of the house. I watch him while I do needlepoint, sitting by the window. He has soaked dried corn in water and plants the kernels in rows he has dug. He bends to the ground making rows for the seeds. It would seem to be backbreaking work.

Returning to the house from the seminary, I suddenly smell the bitter, pungent odor of mangoes. The big mango tree near our house is loaded with yellowish-green balls. There are two types of mango-bearing trees. From one tree you cannot eat the fruit because it tastes like turpentine. Papaya are again ripening on a tree in our back yard. Soon Moses will lay several on the old washing machine on our back porch. He knows when they are ripe for picking.

Tonight the Gaventas come for a visit. We talk about our travel plans for going homeward in May.

Friday, March 10th

I find candles and matches by the light of the torch, light one in the dining area where we eat. This morning Price comes into the kitchen and says he has a brutal headache. I think he's working too hard without much diversion. He studies every day preparing for classes as though he had never taught before. And he has many one-on-one conferences with students here. I urge him to stay in and rest today, but he would have to be really sick not to meet his class.

I get out a strand of beads, made up of old Portuguese trading beads, bought in the marketplace. They are long and round, each almost an inch in length. The colors are light blue, navy, yellow, and white, all intermingled together. I wonder how many hands touched these beads. The Portuguese were in West Africa as early as 1441. Read a book from the seminary library with a highly interesting account of this period of history. Apparently, the Portuguese found several cities in West Africa bigger than any but the largest on their own continent. When they arrived, they saw kingdoms comparable to European states, complex cultures, interesting architecture, domesticated animals, and skilled workers in iron, wood, and brass.

The African slave trade was growing when Europeans arrived. Prisoners of war became slaves of their enemies. It then became a profitable business.

Stories are told here of families who fled and hid from their captors, sometimes never to be found. But the sad truth is that when the slave trade was at its height, the black man profited also, by turning in his own people to the slave traders.

I work today without stopping, going from one task to another, writing, grading papers, proofreading material for the student magazine. By evening and time for dinner at Frances Jones, I am weary. Going into the dining room I see Matthew's lovely flower arrangement of pink hibiscus, coral bells, and white lilies. A small act, but what a lift this beauty brings to my spirits.

Saturday, March 11th

The sun shines palely this morning. Today is our daughter's birthday. My thoughts are wending their way on a long journey to her, along with my prayers. This only daughter of ours, Sara Leslie, whom we call "Poo," is soon to be the mother of her third child in May, in addition to two boys who are six and four years old. She carries a weight of cosmic sadness with her and has since as an eight-year-old she sat in her small black rocking chair and sang "Through the Majesties of Yonder," her own composition. Older now, she writes poetry, transmitting to paper her deep thoughts about things that matter. She is endowed with a sparkling mind, a loving heart and a capacity for unbounded joy.

In the late afternoon Price and I go for a walk, taking our camera to make pictures of the seminary buildings, grounds, and the hospital. The pictures will show only a smattering of what has been experienced here. Yes, there is our house set back from the dusty road and the teak trees around it. But no one seeing this picture can hear the leaves rustling or the drums beating in the night or the sound of our watchman's whistle. All this I will have to carry in my memory and in my heart forever and, in the same way, the faces of those I teach here. So it is that this place for me will never change or any of the people I have known ever grow older, after we leave. So many of our happy times never die but remain lovely memories for us always.

Nearing the house, we see an elderly woman, her back bent, her head toward the ground, carrying a heavy load of firewood across her back. She dips her knee in curtsy to us. I hand her money. I try to control my emotions when I see sorrowful sights, but I hope I am never unmoved by them.

Sunday, March 12th

What does it mean to be honest with oneself? I ponder the question on this early morning, sitting by the window watching the creeping light of a new day. Here in Ogbomosho, I feel I can be more myself. The people I am around are less pretentious, causing me to be more honest about who I am.

The letters of Isak Dinesen contain questions about being oneself. It was a matter that puzzled her also. In a letter, written in 1928 from her home in Africa to her mother in Denmark, she writes, "To be oneself is not as easy as one might think. Many people find it hard to be themselves because there really is not anything in them to be. It is really too much to ask of them, and the best they can do is to find some scraps of philosophy and understanding they have picked up here and there. . . . I think that here (Africa) it comes naturally to me to be myself to be what I believe 'God meant when he made me'. In my relationship with the natives, with white people . . . I believe that I am 'myself as the whole man, the true, with God's sigil (approval) upon my brow'. And that, I believe, is to be happy, to feel like a fish in the water or a bird in the air. And then think that unless one is oneself one cannot do anything much for others."

In Nigeria one is stripped bare of all those comforts and luxuries thought necessary for survival. One has to deal with the interior person and who one is. Truly, I am grateful to know a time in my life like these months.

Later in the morning, I watch a woman walking along the dusty road in front of our house. She spreads her arms wide, laughing and talking to the child she carries on her back. I can hear the child's merry laugh and answer, "Ho." This mother is a beautiful, uncomplicated picture to me of a person being her true self, enjoying a morning walk with her child. I cherish the memory after she passes out of sight down the road.

Monday, March 13th

Everything outdoors looks freshly washed after last night's heavy rain. Again the rain was of short duration but pounded the earth. I am considerably surprised about these tropical rains. I thought when the rainy season began we would have rain day and night for a week at a time. Instead, the rains come up suddenly in late afternoon or night, beating heavily into the ground, and never last more than half an hour.

So many evenings at Frances Jones we meet interesting persons who are staying there briefly as guests. Tonight at dinner a Jamaican woman dines with us. She is married to a wealthy Nigerian and has come to Baptist Hospital for Martha to deliver her baby. She tells us a long and fascinating story about a man from Germany who came to work in Nigeria, took bribes, and got rich. At one time he had 500,000 Naira, invested it, lost all but 50,000 Naira, which he could not prove was his. He was ordered by his German company to go work in a remote part of South America. The Jamaican woman says he reminded her of the rich man who pulled down his barns to build bigger barns. She is a good storyteller, sitting at the table in her colorful Nigerian long dress, head wrapped in a gele, gesticulating, and laughing gleefully.

Tuesday, March 14th

A real day of days! Seven letters for us today (three from our children) in our mail slot in the faculty lounge. What letters can do for the soul when one is so far away. Letters are always a source of comfort for me. I regret that letter-writing is becoming a lost art. The telephone is a poor substitute. Letter writers become personal, often expressing inner feelings in their writing that they find awkward to articulate over the phone.

This morning in English class I teach the words "eyebrow" and "eyelash" to the women. They have no similar word in their tribal languages. Apparently they have never given any name but "eye" to this part of the face, not bothering to signify separately the eyebrow or eyelash. One day I learned that the women did not know how the earth revolves around the sun, or that when it is night in Africa, it is morning somewhere else in the world. When I tried to illustrate all this by a rough drawing on the blackboard, I could tell by the looks on the women's faces that they were overcome with a sense of dread and awe. Several women moaned in a low tone of voice, as if to say, "How frightening."

Wednesday, March 15th

Now at home the first yellow jonquils are blooming. There the smells of spring are in the air, and the sunshine lies softly on your cheek. I miss the feel of springtime. Sultry heat is returning here since the rains have stopped.

80

Price and I awake with headaches. Neither of us slept well. The air lies like a wool blanket over my face. Even the one ceiling fan in the living room stirs up hot air. I sit by the window hoping for a breeze. A ripe mango thuds to the ground. Far off I hear the high wailing muezzin, the Muslim call to prayer. Muslims are in Ogbomosho but predominate farther north. Daylight is a bewitching time.

The town is without water again because of some malfunction of the reservoir machinery. A big cistern back of Frances Jones supplies relief for a few people who walk there, carrying away heavy buckets of water on their heads. One old woman ambled down the road this morning, a pail of water sitting on a pad on top of her head. She shuffled one foot in front of the other, pain and weariness etching her face. I get angry seeing how hard life is for women here.

This evening we are having a birthday party for one of the men teachers who eats dinner with us at Frances Jones. Our dinner is special—chicken curry with rice and tomatoes, groundnuts, coconut, fresh oranges and pineapples. Marjorie has been storing up food for this dinner. Only a week ago, supplies in the kitchen were so low that we finished our light meal by eating peanut butter sandwiches as a supplement.

Thursday, March 16th

A strange, stormy-looking sky this morning, which gradually clears. The sun is shining by 9:00 A.M. Alice comes by with food items. I tease her and accuse her of being a genie, like Aladdin's, who rubs her hands and wishes for food she obtains.

We go to a special program at the seminary tonight and hear a former magician speak, one who has been converted to Christianity. The term, magician, as used here, is another word for wizard or one who practices the occult, the spirit world or evil. This man says he would go to the cemetery to invoke his power. Wizards have the power to cause the death of a person, so most Nigerians believe, through a curse on the individual's life. Strange, strange the things he said. What the man talked about was the students' world and where they come from, a long way back. Many of these students know realistically about the occult.

The man speaks for an hour and thirty minutes and is talking when we leave. His English is not easy to understand. The bench on which we sit is hard, the room is hot, and Price and I are weary. In the inky darkness of night, walking to our house I can understand the power of the occult over people in this land. What unnatural evil lurks in the dark out there?

"What do you make of all that talk?" I ask Price, wondering what or who may be behind the tall bush we pass.

Price has been thinking about the man's talk because his answer is really a speech. "I believe that we live in a dynamic or 'living' universe. I believe that the whole of life is linked in a single chain and that there are powers and mysteries inaccessible to either science or faith. This is what makes possible the appearance of reality in wizardry. So we do not actually know. That answer, in my own mind, is modified by the apparent fact that in cultures where wizards are believed, their powers seem real; and in cultures without such preoccupation, their powers seem manipulatory."

"So again, like many other questions, we do not actually know the answer do we?" I conclude. "It's a puzzlement, like the King of Siam thought in the play, 'The King and I'."

Friday, March 17th

Last night I slept with the scent of a gardenia in a vase by my bedside. A few are blooming on a bush in the flower bed at Frances Jones. We were out in the yard after dinner looking heavenward at the dazzling stars. Martha plucked a gardenia for me. Its fragrance is like nothing else in the world and always brings a reminder of my wedding day, when I carried a bouquet of twelve gardenia blossoms. I awoke this morning to the heady, almost overpowering odor of this one velvety white blossom.

Mangoes are full ripe. Since they last only a few weeks, there is great excitement, as people rush to gather baskets full. The best way to eat this fruit is to stand over a sink and let the mango juice run down, while you smash your mouth into the pulp around the large, hard seed.

Another surveyor from Poland is eating dinner with us at Frances Jones. He has been in the Gobi Desert in Mongolia and also worked near the North Pole. He does not speak English as well as Lech. Too bad!

Saturday, March 18th

Today I begin to fantasize about hamburgers and ice cream cones. Food supplies are daily getting more scarce.

Most mission people go somewhere only because they need to go on business or emergency. No conveniences of sanitary restaurants or rest stops exist. There is no place to go for a relaxing weekend. We do want to see as many different regions of Nigeria as possible, however. None of the faculty can believe we would travel merely to sightsee.

We plan to leave the first of April on a long journey north as far as the Yankari Game Reserve, stopping in the towns of Kaduna, Zaria, Kano, and Jos along the way. Already I am giving myself pep talks in an effort to work up courage for this trip.

Sunday, March 19th

It is amazing, when I walk about on the campus and along the corridors by the classrooms, go to chapel, or pass by the students housing quarters, how much liveliness is evident. Students meet and talk with much laughter. I am impressed that I hardly ever see taut, strained expressions on their faces. The women move with cat-like grace from years of balancing heavy loads on their heads. The men talk with animated faces. Many of the men and women are fine looking, having large, expressive eyes and a gentle, almost defensive glance.

As Laurels Van der Post said of Africans, "their laughter seems to come straight from some sure, inviolate source within where one felt they were unfailingly refreshed. Their laughter matched the sun, the curve of a sky, and the somberly burning land. . . ."

When the students sing together in chapel, their voices are strong and rhythmical. Most of the group appear happy, except for the wives on days when they look weary. Since theirs is a land where the unexpected is always occurring, they like for something to be happening. I believe these people would become desperate tied to a nine-to-five routine existence. The have lived a great part of their lives outdoors, near the forest or jungle growth or on the uncluttered plains. To be enclosed by office walls or modern buildings, without windows, would surely make them miserable.

We wake up to a sultry morning, the sun already blazing. Nat is filling tubs with water, ready to do our week's wash. He must enjoy scrubbing clothes clean. He smiles and sings all the while.

This afternoon we are invited to the opening ceremonies of the *Sohun's* new palace, really a large, concrete blockhouse in the middle of the town. The *Sohun*, pronounced Shawn, is like the mayor of a town, only here he is the tribal chief, or minor king.

When we arrive, there is a state of elegant confusion everywhere. So much is happening one cannot view all the spectacles! Some 1,000 villagers gather inside the courtyard surrounding the *Sohun's* new residence and outside the walls, along the road.

A trumpet fanfare announces the *Sohun's* arrival. Five trumpeters, garbed in red tunics and pants, stand on the roof of a nearby building. The *Sohun* proceeds into the courtyard. Walking on each side of him are men holding gold and maroon-striped opened umbrellas, twice the size of beach umbrellas. These umbrellas shade the *Sohun* as he walks. Resting on top of one umbrella is a carved wooden lion and on the other, a carved wooden elephant. Two other men fan the *Sohun* with enormous, peacock-feathered fans. Traveling behind the *Sohun* are his four wives, dressed and veiled in white. The crowd of men and women spectators wear "fine, fine" clothes in every hue of the rainbow. Most of the women have on from six to seven gold bracelets, long gold earrings, and necklaces.

We enter all this array and are led to seats on an overstuffed couch, placed under a long tent on the sidelines, where guests sit in the shade. We are to be honored guests. On the platform to the left of us, a man is delivering an oration in Yoruba—apparently a mixture of wisdom and humor. But in front of us a man turns somersaults in the air to entertain the crowd. He stops long enough to speak to a Muslim leader sitting nearby. This man is wrapped in a red velvet, gold-encrusted robe. The heat must be 100 degrees in the shade. He does not sweat.

Suddenly another trumpet blast heralds the arrival of more elaborately dressed dignitaries on horseback. Drummers beat their dust-covered leather drums, decorated on each end with gold bells shaped like long vases. In the midst of this pageantry, a young Nigerian man comes to introduce himself to us. He speaks excellent English. No wonder! He recently returned to Nigeria after graduating from Bowman Gray Medical School in North Carolina.

When we leave through the ornate iron gates opening from the courtyard to the street, a crowd of Ogbomosho hunters, the town's most honored men, rush to follow us, firing their old flintlock rifles into the air. We jump back from the explosive noise. They laugh heartily. Whether it was meant to be a joke or their way of saying good-bye, we do not know. It is a time of high jinx and revelry. A "great, great" afternoon.

Tuesday, March 21st

A fine, fine morning a la Nigeria. Birds are singing, daylight is breaking.

Gloria comes to work later in the morning. I am grading papers from women in the English class. These women are beginning to write sentences in good English. I am proud of them. I stop my work to talk with Gloria. She is worried because David, her husband, has an upset stomach. I give her some tea bags and tell her how to make hot tea for him. I urge her to persuade him to drink the tea, but she looks skeptical, I can tell.

When Price comes from his office we have toast, boiled eggs and guava jelly for lunch. Price's trader woman comes by with a load of large avocados. Their flesh is more green than yellow, and the taste is more bitter than Florida or California ones.

I walk to my office for a conference with a student from the writing class. He is the most poorly prepared in English of all the students in class, but he is earnestly sincere and is trying with all his ability. I help him today with difficult English expressions. As he leaves, he thanks and thanks me, bowing from the waist down. Imagine a student in the States doing that out of respect for a teacher.

The electricity is off again tonight. No radio, or reading, or doing needlepoint. We sit and talk together by candlelight in the quiet room. I know I will long for uncluttered evenings like this when we return home.

Wednesday, March 22nd

The morning sun today is scalding. I want to flee its wrath. It seems to sear my skin, penetrate my head, and make me dizzy.

85

I hurry along the path from the Women's Building to reach our house for cover. Even the frangipani blossoms look pinched and dry. The rainy season did not last long enough to help the arid, hard ground. The bold, intense color of flowers—red, purple, sharp yellow, salmon pink, and purest white—stand out vividly in the fiery, bright sunshine. Sometimes my heart cries out for respite from so much rich abundance.

Late afternoon and Martha and Alice are calling for us to come outdoors. We go to the back porch and see the two women standing in the yard, holding a dead green mamba snake on the end of a long stick. They laugh merrily and yell that they did not want us to return home without having seen a snake in Africa. Price and I have a good laugh, too. I have heard so many gruesome tales of snakes since being here—how they wait in ambush to strike—that I am relieved to see this dead one!

Odd what concepts people have of foreign places they have never visited. Price's barber in Greenville, when he learned we were going to Africa, declared he would "never set foot in that country because there were too many snakes." Price talked one day in Greenville with a Nigerian student who had come to study at Greenville Tech. This man told Price that a South Carolina woman asked him if his people still lived in trees. Then Marjorie tells the story of being home on furlough and speaking to a women's group about her work in Nigeria. At the end of her talk, Marjorie said that the next week she would be returning to Nigeria. One of the women asked the question, "Will you be driving through?"

Thursday, March 23rd

Some days are leaden like this one. I suppose this may be because Shirley, who lives next door, is leaving tomorrow for the States on a brief furlough. I long to go with her, stay for a week's visit, then return here. I am daydreaming, of course. Just an hour's visit with each of our children would surely help, only to see their faces and look into their eyes.

Living isolated from cultural events requires imagination to provide one's own entertainment, as those know who have lived here a long time. Tonight Martha is having an Easter celebration at Frances Jones. Some 25 people come during the evening. Altogether there is quite a diversity with chaplain, interns, doctors, teachers, mission personnel, and our two Polish surveyor friends. We are like one family, united in a meaningful way. In such a faraway place, the desire for community is more heartfelt, I believe, and I have a sense we are not giving to others all the time, but people are giving back to us, filling our lives too.

Friday, March 24th

No classes today because of the Easter holiday weekend. Easter is observed by the seminary staff and in the Ogbomosho Baptist churches.

This morning Thomas' wife, Anna, is coming to get several skirts and blouses and a dress I am giving her. She is tall, slender, and regal-looking, with a profile resembling that of Nefertiti of Egypt. In my class she sometimes seems sullen and haughty. She and Thomas have five children and are taking care of his brother's child. The older brother in a family is expected to care for the younger brother's children, if the younger brother is not secure financially. Thomas has the grandest smile of any student here. Unlike Anna, he laughs readily and is in a happy mood whenever you see him. Anna's English is limited, but Thomas speaks fluently and enunciates English words distinctly. It is difficult to estimate the relationship between student husbands and wives. There is no hugging, hand-holding, or touching publicly. Thomas and Anna are a handsome couple. I hope they are happy together.

Anna comes to the door for the clothes. I invite her inside. She is quiet and shy, seeming almost afraid to enter. I would ask her to try on the clothes to see if they fit before she takes them, but I know she would not want to do this. So I show her each garment, then fold them into a bundle for her. She smiles warmly, looks pleased, and thanks me. Then she departs out the door in a hurry, not looking back. Nonetheless, I have a feeling the African, in an unexplainable way, recognizes the character of each of us strangers.

The groundnut trader woman comes by. I buy two pounds of unshelled groundnuts. She shells them for me by pouring them in a flat pan, pitching the pan high in the air, and catching them. Then, with her hands she rubs off the hulls that have broken loose until she has all the peanuts shelled. This woman must be in her 70s; her skin is creased and wrinkled. She has been selling peanuts on the campus for many, many years, Alice says. I like her spirit. She takes her peanut shelling job seriously in a pleasant, no-nonsense way.

Saturday, March 25th

Where should I begin this morning? I start thinking about what has to be done this day. Always I have to think about what we'll eat for lunch, trying to improvise a meal from whatever may be in the fridge. We are losing weight, which is OK. I have yet to see an obese Nigerian, of the type person so frequently seen in the States.

In the midst of doing my chores, I am aware of how one loses all sense of time out here, not only of time but sense of distance. Both time and distance seem to merge. Perhaps it is because I think often of things far away, and I somehow feel those people and places are doing the same things as the way I remember them when I left. It is difficult for me to explain, but this can give me a strange feeling.

We eat lunch and I leave to go visit a new mother (student wife) at the hospital, taking an orange and some candy mints I have saved. I find her joyful over the birth of her first daughter.

I return to our house by walking to the front of the hospital which faces the highway. From there I walk on the shoulder of the highway past small mud houses and rusted tin-roofed enclosures for goats. I remind myself that as ugly as this scene is, it is far better than the terrible hell on earth I viewed several years ago when we drove through the worst part of New York City's inner ghetto. Gutted buildings and burned out cars everywhere and the hard, empty faces of people who had given up. No life there. No one has given up here, and the faces of most people reflect that they still possess a mind, a spirit, and soul.

Sunday, March 26th

I was at work before daylight this morning writing another story for the Greenville News. This one is about the elegant confusion of the dedication of the town chief's palace.

Today we take Alice with us and go to a Yoruba-speaking church in Ogbomosho. We drive down a twisting dirt road, past mud houses and much debris of garbage here and there in piles along the roadside. When we park the car and walk toward the church, children rush toward us, wanting to shake our hands. Seeing white people is still strange to small children here and they want to touch our flesh. Often children call out to us, *oyingbo*, which means "peeled or skinned ones." They do this playfully, not in an ugly manner.

We enter the large church already filled with people. The women's rainbow-colored geles, massed together as they sit row after row, resemble a Persian carpet. The most dressed up ones want to sit up front to be seen, Alice says. I am amused by the way people pack the pews. If the pew seems already full, others will shove and push their way in until room is made for them to sit down. Children wander up and down the aisles, many carrying babies on their hips.

The worship service begins with a women's choir singing in front on one side and a youth choir singing on the opposite side. They sing for ten minutes, swaying to the rhythm of drum beats and a wooden clacking sound. The youths move their feet and step to each beat of the music, in a dancing way. A man comes to the pulpit, holding a small child aloft in his arms an speaks in Yoruba. Alice says that, since the child is lost, the man is inquiring about the parents.

Suddenly a group of young children—eight to twelve years of age—come dancing and swaying down the aisle by our seats, led by a young woman dancing backwards. They are going to the front of the church with their Easter offering. The music and drumbeats get louder. A minister prays for ten minutes.

The sermon is an hour long. Then there is more singing, swaying, and clapping in tune to the music as the service ends. So much joy is expressed that I, too, am in a joyful, grateful-for-life mood when we leave the church this day.

Monday, March 27th

Today we are to visit a Fulani tribe and a village market with J. W. Richardson.

At 6:00 A.M., I am up making cheese sandwiches to take with us on our trip to the savannah country. We go to J. W.'s house, climb into his Land Rover, and begin our ride ten miles or so down the highway. I am happy when we turn off into a narrow dirt road that takes us through scrubby bush land. We ride and ride until we come literally to the end of the road. J. W. leaves the car locked, and we begin walking a path through the tall, pale cream-colored grass to the Fulani people. After walking several miles, we sight a herd of cows, some fifty in all, grazing in grassy clumps near thatched-roof, round grass huts.

Women appear, wrapped in dark pieces of cloth, their wrists encircled with six or seven wide, heavy, silver bracelets. Naked children come shyly out of the huts. Some of the children have sores on their heads or bodies. As they gather closer to us, I see that the older women have tattoos on faces and arms. They wear their hair in long plaits on either side their faces. A few of the women wear heavy, wide, brass bracelets halfway up their arms.

We sit with J. W. on a straw mat under a small tree. He plays a tape recording in Hausa about the gospel story and, at the same time, shows pictures in a book of what the tape is saying in words. Several women and children sit on the mat beside us. I wonder how long it has been since these people bathed, yet I don't smell any foul odors. Flies swarm everywhere, some crawling on the children's faces. The Fulani's principal food is milk and cheese. No men ever come to the mat.

In the car again, we drive to a large, sprawling market, like a flea market at home, five miles away. Expertly woven straw baskets sell for 40 cents (US). I find and buy a string of old Portuguese trading beads. My most prized possession from that day is a tiny straw basket, used as a cheese strainer, given to me by a Fulani man, as we left his village. It will remind me always of the Fulani, so far away in time and place.

Tuesday, March 28th

I am not sleeping well again. The nights are swelteringly humid and drums are beating more often, somewhere near.

Alice brings us cinnamon rolls for breakfast this morning. She laughs and says they are made with flour that had bugs in it. The bugs were sifted out, she reports, and the heat of the oven, in which they were baked, makes them safe for eating. What people here learn to tolerate! Hazel Moon told us that, when the well was drained from which she was getting water at her place, three dead rats were found at the bottom. Ugh! She said she was sick that week, but recovered!

Several women did not come to class today. They were sick from eating too many mangoes. When mangoes ripen, many persons are greedy and overeat.

I take a long walk before dinner. I think of a dear friend of thirty years' friendship. We have not lived near each other for fifteen years, yet, when we see each other, all is the same. Human communication in this world is so difficult. It is not easy to get to know another person, and this is becoming increasingly so in our present day culture. How rare to find a person who has thoughts similar to your own. Usually people seek to engage in surface talk only.

Wednesday March 29th

Gloria will not come to work today. She has a child sick with boils, another child with ear infection. She is depressed because the children are always sick. I think it is because their diet is not a good one. Their food and most of the students' food consists of too much cassava, a starchy tuberous plant, yams, beans with scrawny chicken meat or tough beef. They eat fruit only when it is in season, like banana, papaya, mango, or pineapple. Gloria said once to me that she would like to go to America to live. I tried to explain to her such a move would not necessarily make her happy. I imagine she thinks all her cares would vanish in such a land of plenty.

Westerners do seem extremely well off compared to Gloria's standard of living. Because many Nigerians believe that "he who has knowledge is good," what a shock for them to discover this is not necessarily so in our country of higher education and culture. I do not encourage Gloria to make such a great leap. When her husband graduates from the seminary this May, she and the children will return with him to an Ibo village, their homeland. He will pastor a church there. While life will continue to be hard, for them it will be best. Probably in America no community would provide a strong support group nor the sense of belonging they will have always in their familiar village.

On a morning like this one, I long to be outside working in

flower gardens. My garden, like my church, is a place of reassurance along with a place for retreat. A garden speaks to me of death and rebirth and survival in a world of impermanence.

Thursday, March 30th

Earlier at 5:00 A.M. this morning, a rainstorm descended and the electricity cut off. In the monochromatic morning light, trees and bushes look defined in shape and outlines. I breathe more deeply drafts of fresh air coming through the windows, like drinking water from a cold mountain stream, the refreshment of it.

The mission people who were the first on this compound in the late 1800s and early 1900s were farsighted enough to plant flowering trees and bushes. New pots of flowering plants are kept along the open corridors that connect the seminary chapel to the classroom buildings on both sides. Old Ba Ba, the gardener, waters and tends these plants. How cold and stark the look would be without their color and foliage.

Somehow too spiritless today to write more.

Friday, March 31st

Slept until 6:40 A.M., later than usual, but last night was quiet with no drums and no heavy trucks on the road changing gears. Nat arrives at 7:00 A.M. on his bicycle, fills the tubs outside with water, and starts scrubbing clothes. He is neat and orderly, moving from washing tub to rinsing tub with no extra splashes of water on the ground. I like the way he works with no wasted motion.

Matthew comes from Frances Jones bringing a large banana stalk with twenty bananas on it. I will take bananas to the women in my English class.

Price leaves in a Peugeot, with Carl driving, to go over the potholed road to Oshogbo. He has to get a registry card for us, something required by the Nigerian government before we can leave their country. The Peugeot is a comfortable car, but even so, on every road but the main highway, you bounce up and down on the seats and hang onto whatever is available.

We go to prayer meeting at 5:00 P.M. I gaze at the faces of nurses, teachers, doctors, administrators—most are tired. I am struck, however, time and time again by their look of peace and contentment. I never fail to be inspired being among them.

Tonight at Frances Jones, the table is set on the front screen porch. A lovely, soft breeze blows while we all sit together. Outside the sky is inky black, no stars out, no moon. Candlelight dances in the breeze. I smell the heady, sweet odor of lilies in Martha's garden.

I tell myself, "yes, you are in Africa and it is good to be here." Hardly the way I felt in January. Someone mentions that inflation is up in the US and television programs are worse than ever. I find myself not caring about the news. Tomorrow we leave on our long trip by car to northern Nigeria.

APRIL

Saturday, April 1st

We are astir at 5:30 A.M. I slept lightly after 3:00 A.M. Too excited about leaving on our trip north today but fearful, too, about the highways We will be riding all day toward Zaria by way of Kaduna and other towns. Carl and Enid are taking us in the Peugeot. After breakfast, I make cheese sandwiches and stuff bananas in the bag with them; Enid is bringing sandwiches and bottled filtered water. We must take our own toilet paper, mosquito repellent, bandages, and antiseptic spray, and the ever necessary torch. There'll be no sanitary eating places or restrooms along the way. Enid instructs me about how we will make a "necessary" rest stop.

"Carl will stop the car on the shoulder of the road near a forest or tall bush area," she says, "and we'll head for the bush by couples."

I laugh and tell her that suits me fine because I certainly don't want to go there by myself. How easy it is to take for granted the fairly well-kept rest areas along the highways at home.

While I am packing clothes to take, I keep thinking about the four small boys who played with the drummer who performed for all of us at Frances Jones last night. Two adult men stood by the drummer and rattled the shakee-shakees. Children beat the long drums slung over their shoulder by a strap. Their faces were solemn and expressionless, but the rhythm was unmistakably African. They beat out our names on the talking drums. Then we all danced around with the drummers while they played their drums. Actually it was more like stomping our feet and waving our arms! Drums of the dundun set have two membranes connected by leather thongs. By pressing the thongs with his left hand the drummer can change the pitch of the drum.

After the dancing, one of the drummers left and walked a distance away in the front yard. Another drummer had Martha take off one of her shoes and hide it in the living room. The drummers talked on their drums back and forth to each other. Then the man in the yard came inside and found the shoe where Martha hid it behind the couch.

At 7:00 A.M. Price and I are ready. We drive to the Whirley's house, leave our car there, and together we pack our gear and theirs into their car. The sky is a dismal light gray as we drive out of the seminary entrance. I say a prayer for safekeeping. We head toward Ilorin, north up the highway. Ten miles from Ogbomosho, we pass a wrecked truck with its cargo of cattle dead and dying in the ditch by the highway. The smell is so bad, we have to drive with the windows closed for several minutes. Farther on we drive by a wrecked lorry with several dead people lying beside the road. Cars have stopped and people are bending to look at the bodies. There is nothing we can do but exclaim, "Oh how terrible!"

Late morning, we begin to see different kinds of villages, all enclosed with straw fences, square mud houses with straw thatched roofs, scrubby trees, heavy undergrowth, and clearings scratched out in the undergrowth where someone is trying to grow food. Seven-and-eight-foot-tall ant hills, looking like miniature Gothic churches, dot the dry patches of land where low underbrush grows. We cross the wide brass-colored Niger River and drive toward the town of Bida. The countryside is again changing. I begin to see hills in the distance, round high rock formations, and expansive stretches of green trees, palms and eucalyptus, and scarlet blossoms of flame trees. Oh, lovely sight!

Coming into Bida, Carl finds a government-run way station. He stops the car under the shade of a tree in the round driveway of this place. We eat our lunch standing up, with the trunk of the car our table. Some white-breasted, black crows circle overhead, cawing raucously while we eat. The air is stifling hot and humid. Carl says we cannot go inside the government place because it is too unsanitary. A man comes from one building carrying a jug of water and offers it to Carl for us to drink. Everyone but me takes a drink of this water. The jug looks dirty. Carl says he had to take the water or the man would be offended. Sure enough, Price and Enid are sick with diarrhea a day later. (Carl isn't but says he has an iron stomach.) Carl hires an old man to guide us to the village craft shops.

Bida, the center where the Nupe people live, is known for its local crafts of brassworkers, glassworkers, blacksmiths, and women cloth-weavers. The Nupe people live in densely-populated settlements around the Niger River. Their houses, scattered along the fertile plains, are collections of round, plain mud buildings within enclosing mud walls, breached by an entrance room. Inside the walls, houses normally contain a room for each wife, a room for unmarried daughters, one for unmarried sons, an inner entrance room for visitors, a man's room, and a stable and granaries, small buildings on raised stones.

We go along a dirt alleyway between mud houses in a village following our guide, to a small room where a woman is weaving cloth on a loom. Generally, the women work on broadlooms. There is little influence on this craft from the outside, except for imported dyes and yarns sometimes used. I like the black and red pattern she is making. I offer to buy the cloth but she doesn't want to sell. We turn to leave, and the woman comes running after me to sell the piece, which I buy.

From there we walk to the hot and menacing-looking glass blower's hut. Glass beads for ornamentation have been made in Bida for many centuries. Old glass beads, agate and coral, can still be found in the village markets. Now old bottles are used as raw material, particularly Guiness beer bottles for brown glass, Star beer bottles for green glass, and Milk of Magnesia bottles for a rich midnight blue.

The place we enter is a small, round hut with a few tiny windows. The furnace is an open fire within low mud walls in the center of a concrete floor. The fire is kept red hot by a man pumping a handmade bellows made of goat skins. Two men melt the glass and shape the soft mass into bangles or beads with the help of two iron rods, sometimes mixing two or more different colored pieces of glass. The men are naked from the waist up. It is like a scene in an inferno—I don't know which is hotter, the inside of the hut or the day outside. I am about faint from the terrific heat. I go outside and breathe deeply for air. Price leaves right behind me, saying he's had enough of that. His face is flushed and red.

In another hut, a giant of a man sits on a dirt floor pounding and beating brass into pots, jars, and figures. Everything being made is for sale, as well as strands of glass beads. One necklace of terra cotta-colored beads catches my eye and Price buys it for me.

When we walk to the car, eight or ten men traders follow us, their arms strung with strands of beads. They want us to buy more. The men push and shove each other, trying to get at us. One man rams a necklace toward my face, then tries to place it around my neck. I am unnerved by all this chaos and heat. We reach the car and I plunge inside. Carl and Enid are surprised at these men being so aggressive.

We drive on through flat country, not many trucks on the highway. In the distance I see Fulani wandering with their cows or sheep. I like the peaceful look of this high country. We near Kaduna in late afternoon and must continue to drive almost fifty miles more to Zaria. There we and the Whirleys will be the guests of the Bert Dysons, missionaries in that area. It does not rain in this region from October through May; the parched and reddish earth is crusty and cracked.

Nearing dark, we pull into the driveway of Bert and Ruth Dyson's home. Their house, resembling an American ranch-style house, has a spacious green lawn in front, trees, and flowers everywhere. I cannot believe what I am seeing is in Nigeria.

We have a king-sized bed for sleeping. Roses bloom in the back yard and birds sing.

I sleep soundly until early morning when I hear angry voices exchanging words nearby. Some Zaria people are arguing on a road in front of the house. When all is quiet again, I lie awake listening to a strange bird call. We are deep in the heart of Muslim country, I suddenly remember. Then faraway I hear the muezzin call to prayer—the plaintive cry always recognizable. Strange bird, strange prayer, strange times!

Sunday, April 2nd

Looking out the window, I see a bird feeder where pinkish gray pigeons are pecking and a gorgeous, blackish-iridescent blue bird hops on the ground. Through the open windows of our bedroom, a cool, pleasant breeze billows the white curtains. Roses of pink and yellow hues bloom near the corner of the house. I have a sense of well-being standing here, one of those unexplainable times that come, often unexpectedly, to anyone when life seems so good and right. A small epiphany.

Price and I go with the Dysons after breakfast to a Hausa compound for worship at a Hausa-speaking Baptist church. We walk through narrow streets bounded on each side by small houses built of mud blocks. An elderly man and a small boy, ten or eleven years old, sit with their backs to the wall of a house. The old man is instructing the boy in copying words from the Koran, using a writing pen made of bamboo. Both smile from happy-looking faces.

The modest church building is built of mud blocks, painted white. We sit in the rear of the church on hard wooden benches with no backs. I look outside the open windows on one side and see a bougainvillaea bush, large as a tree, heavy with pink blossoms.

Five Hausa women wearing long, colorful skirts and blouses, and gold jewelry go to the front, each carrying a gourd with a hole in the sides, and pound with the palms of their hands on the sides of the *calabash* gourds. Another woman stands in front and directs the group.

Their music sounds like a mixture of drum beat and the noise of someone blowing through a hole. We go outside after more that an hour of sitting. My back aches and my head throbs under the glaring, sickeningly-hot sun. I know I am tired from the trip and need some rest. Price looks droopy, but he shakes hands with men to whom Dyson introduces us.

After lunch I take a long nap. Price has diarrhea from drinking the strange water in Bida. He decides to stay in Zaria, and I leave with the Whirleys and Dysons at 3:00 P.M. for Kaduna and the meeting of the Nigerian Baptist Convention, held in a soccer stadium. Carl says there will be some 5,000 Nigerians coming for this convention, mostly from Yoruba and Hausa speaking tribes. We sit in the stadium under the broiling sun.

Finally, we leave the meeting, driving in the dark over dangerous roads. We stop once, abruptly, because there is a donkey in the middle of the highway. The darkness brings no relief from the heat. Somehow, the sultriness this evening is worse than ever in Ogbomosho. When we return to the Dyson's house, we find Price is much better.

Monday, April 3rd

Sleeping under a fan in Zaria. Cool breezes blow in the night, so we turn off the fan. Strange that the air is sultry and heavy when we go to bed. From where does this cool air arrive?

Today everyone goes to the meeting in Kaduna, except Price and I. We linger, eating a late breakfast, savoring the morning to ourselves. We read, then walk outside, looking at the flowering rose bushes. A delightful place to be. Later we ride, with a Nigerian driver, to a museum in Zaria where local craftsmen work. Zaria is one of the original seven Hausa states and is several centuries old. Many of the houses have intriguing designs on their walls, sometimes painted, sometimes molded into the mud or etched with white.

Once at the museum, we look in at small, open-air shops rimming a courtyard in back. Brasswork, cloth weaving, leatherwork, silverwork shops. Inside the museum are tribal masks and masquerade costume pieces from the Iron Age and cleavers from the Stone Age.

We go to the soccer stadium for the afternoon meeting of the Nigerian Baptist Convention. Dr. Dahunsi, executive secretary of the convention, calls Price and me to the stage to be introduced by him to the crowd in the stadium. Price and I are very honored to be presented by him to his people, who stand and applaud us. Dahunsi is much loved by the Nigerian Baptists.

With the Whirleys and Dysons, we leave Kaduna, driving in a heavy rainstorm toward Zaria. First a mighty and gusty wind blows dust in whirlpools across the road in front of the car. Then the rain comes in sheets, the sky lighting up with spectacular flashes of lightning. Abruptly we come upon a truck parked on the highway in front of us, with no lights shining. Carl does a good job of avoiding it. I breathe more easily when we turn in at the gate of the Dysons' home.

Tuesday, April 4th

Early 6:00 A.M. breakfast with Bert Dyson. Then Price and I get into his car, with him driving us northward to the old city of Kano. A walled city originally, Kano is a mixture of ancient and modern, with commercial and industrial centers grown up around the old part. An international airport is located here where the trans-Saharan camel routes once ended! Camel caravans came across the Sahara to Timbuktu, in present day Mali, or toward Kano; there, men would trade and barter goods.

Bert takes water in jugs for us to drink during the day and reminds us that the heat will be worse than in Zaria. Once out of the town, we drive through agricultural land, seeing irrigated farming of tomatoes and onions. We begin to sight strangely-constructed villages in the distance. Painted pieces of clay stick out of the top of mud houses; houses are painted on the outside in weird geometric designs of white or black paint. Mud huts have round tops and underneath a cross beam of woven-reed construction. We pass Fulani along the roadside herding their livestock.

Riding the 100 miles from Zaria to Kano is more like 300 miles, fighting heat and dry wind all the way. Finally, we drive into the ancient part of the city with its sand-colored low buildings looking lost amid the dust and sandy roads, all the same hue. Heat blurs my vision; heat rises in waves from the road. No trees to shelter us, or the car, from the sun. From the parked car, we walk a block or so to a museum. No relief there—the inside is hot and stifling. I look passively at iron weapons once used for splitting a man's skull, at iron doors punctured with bullet holes from British guns, and at a long battle garment decorated with feathers. How could men fight in heat like today?

Out in the glaring light again, Bert drives us to the dye pits where men dye cloth with indigo. The blue dye is concocted from vegetable leaves and other natural matter. Cylindrical pots are built into pits dug in the ground. Each one of the pots is up to a meter in diameter and two and-one-half meters deep. Pots are filled with the dye water and the cloth soaked one or two days there. Then the cloth is rinsed, dried, and stretched taut by two men, who fill their mouths with water and send a fine spray over the cloth, later folding it neatly. One man sits by each pit, naked from the waist up. With their bare hands, the men slosh the cloth up and down in blue-black liquid in the pot. The indigo smells like sulphur or rotten eggs. The temperature is hitting 110 degrees. I begin to feel nauseated and dizzy. I protest that I cannot take any more of these sights and smells in this kind of heat.

Price agrees with me. He hurries us to the car, with Dyson following behind us. Price thinks we need to find a place to rest and to drink something cold. Dyson says we will find a hotel. On the way there, he points toward a road which leads to an open-air market. Dyson says traders from Timbuktu still travel there with exotic wares and wants to know if we would like to go there. As much as I would love seeing the place, both Price and I say, "NO, NO!" We have earlier said no, also, to climbing stairs to the top of the Kano great mosque for a view of the city. The heat saps our energy and any desire to sightsee. I can't remember that this has ever happened before when we have traveled.

We reach a decent looking hotel. "Thank God," I say inwardly. We find a room resembling a restaurant and order glasses of orange juice. Thirty minutes later, a waiter appears with our three glasses of warm, canned orange juice and a bill for $8.00 (US). We drink every drop and laugh at paying such a high price to quench our thirst. By now the water in the car is too hot to drink.

Since orange juice is so expensive at this hotel, Dyson decides for us to try lunch at another place. At the Dalbar Hotel, we find a dining area with white tablecloths on tables and with slight air conditioning. I sink into my seat at the table, too exhausted to talk. Our lunch is broiled tomatoes stuffed with rice, large pieces of strange-looking meat, potatoes, carrots, cabbage, and flan for dessert. I eat all of everything but the meat. Bert and Price eat theirs, even though Bert thinks it may be camel.

This day has been long and tiresome, yet I feel pleased to have endured and survived. In all the journeying we have done in Nigeria, my mind in an eerie way believes the clock has gone awry. We are thousands of years back in time and nothing would surprise me, not even a dinosaur stalking the forest land. I ride the long way returning to Zaria lost in much thinking. Why do the hardships and difficulties of life here in some ways seem more satisfying than the ease of life in the West?

Isak Dinesen wrote that "most people, if they could manage it, would be happier traveling around from one fair to another with a monkey, if that would enable them to gain some experience and have new impressions and movement, than sitting with a secure income in an insured house, where one day is just like another." She thought "that most people have an unconscious feeling that there is more nourishment for soul and spirit in danger and wild hopes and in hazarding everything, than in a calm and secure existence." Dinesen believed that people are "extremely under-nourished in this respect, and would give almost anything to the one who can get them this nourishment." She herself was certainly a "yes-sayer" to life.

Wednesday, April 5th

During the night I hear drums beating and eerie high screams like someone calling for help in desperation. I cannot return to sleep but lie there thinking about child sacrifice that is reported to take place in this country. Price sleeps soundly throughout the night. We are told many children disappear, never to be found again. People think they are taken by members of secret cults, devil worshipers who drink human blood. When I am awake and there is daylight, I can scarcely believe these reports, but in the black dark of an African night, I do.

We leave the Dyson's house at 8:00 A.M. with the Whirleys and drive toward Kaduna. Today I feel like a terrible sinner in comparison to these missionaries I am meeting and living with in Ogbomosho and on our journey north. They never complain about difficulties, never get upset, never criticize, work long hours, and very seldom have weekends for rest or recreation. I am tired, weary of being with such saint-like people. Can they be human, I wonder? I know how much they live in prayer and dependence on God. I, too, want this serenity and peace in spite of stress and strain. Living in Ogbomosho, I can feel more composed. It is the unknown now, where we are traveling, the dangerous highways, the unexplained noises of the nights, the debilitating heaviness of the air—all are taking their toll. I hold my feelings in, except to voice some of them to Price.

In Kaduna we return again to meetings in the soccer stadium. We take a break and go to a Western-style hotel, sit in soft chairs in the lobby and drink good, hot coffee. No one else goes in or out of the lobby during the hour we are there—a very empty place.

Thursday, April 6th

After a morning convention meeting in the stadium, Price and I go with friends to see old British residential areas of Kaduna, where spectacular flame trees bloom.

We eat lunch, then transfer our luggage to Paul Miller's car, after saying goodbye to the Whirleys. For the next three days, we and the Millers will be riding north to Jos and to the Yankari Game Reserve.

For several hours, we travel in lowlands, then climb hills toward a higher elevation. The air is cooler, and we see mountains in the distance, a wonderful sight. It is like seeing a beloved child again after a long absence. I want to shout with joy. Paul says we are going up the escarpment into flat plateau country. Jos is in Plateau State and is 4400 feet above sea level. Over the mountain tops, clouds are rolling and gathering for a rainstorm. When we reach the plateau, vast areas of land stretch as far as my eyes can see. An exhilarating view opens across miles and miles of green fields resembling young wheat in the springtime. Smoke curls upward in the air from a tribal village, far away in the distance. I long to stay and sink deeply into this loveliness.

We push on because of wanting to reach Jos and the mission hostel before dark. Jos is a different looking town, which I sense immediately, as we drive past clean yards in front of houses and shops. Even the streets are in better condition. Children of mission personnel come to Jos to live and to attend a school run especially for them.

We stay here overnight and meet teachers and students at a welcoming dinner. We talk with a couple, recently returned from the game reserve, who saw elephants in the wild when they were there. I hope we have such good luck. I can't believe that the night air is cool enough here for a sweater to feel comfortable.

Friday, April 7th

A filling breakfast this morning at the girls' dining room in the school at Jos. Parents of these students pay a high price for room and board in order for their kids to have good food. Probably worth it in better morale. Outside the dining hall, roses, geraniums, petunias, amaryllis and African daisies bloom. The climate is not as hot here as in the lowlands and flowers grow lushly.

We take a tour of Jos, with the Millers, in their car. An excellent museum here displays a large collection of early African cultures. This museum is the second largest in Nigeria. We see a number of Nok terra cotta figurines and an entire collection of hand-thrown pots from almost every part of the country. Nok sculpture is

106

thought to date to 900 B.C. and 200 A.D. Some of the bronze pots were produced between 600 and 1040 A.D. Terra cotta figures are in animal and human form. The bronzes are nearly all heads, many of which have vertical incisions running down cheeks and curving down under the chin, thought to be an old style of tribal marking. I stand and gaze at an amazing cuff bracelet used in fighting, made of iron with spikes of iron sticking out all around the cuff. I am saddened to think of how long men have been fighting each other using cruel instruments to kill.

Early afternoon we leave on our long drive with the Millers to the Yankari Game Reserve in Bauchi State. Soon we are in hilly and mountainous country, dotted with villages along the way. Fulani are here too, wandering across undulating hills with their cattle. Some scenes are ethereal and dream-like—the light, the distance, the effect of being far away in time past. I sit in the car not wanting to talk, desiring more to allow these vignettes to sink deep in my mind for remembering on other days.

Suddenly, we head into terrible road conditions, deep chuck holes, washed out places, some stretches like an old corrugated washboard. Grimy and gritty sandy dirt swirls ahead of our car, then in the open windows and over us. We drop down from the high plateau and move to lowlands level. Again the sultry heat returns and the oppressive air.

Four miles from our destination, we spot a large gray baboon sitting at the base of a tree. A baboon with blue legs! We pass scrubby bushes, smaller trees, and in the distance we can see a panorama of trees, a dense forest.

Late in the afternoon, we reach the game reserve. Price and I, as do the Millers, rent a private cabin at Wikki, on the grounds near the reserve. The cabin is round-shaped, like the village huts, with a thatched roof, and is air-conditioned! Our beds have mosquito netting to be used for protection during the night. We unpack and put on our bathing suits. It is a short walk down a hill to a warm springs pool in a picturesque setting, shaded by palm trees. Clear water bubbles out from under a sheer sandstone cliff and flows over white sand. The water has a constant temperature of 88 degrees. Looking up at the bank on one side, I see three baboons sitting there, eating a red fruit and watching us. Someone sights a baby crocodile resting in the water by the opposite bank. I keep a wary eye on it, never relaxing again or enjoying the water as much as before.

Our supper in the restaurant is a disaster. We are served lamb with a half-fried egg on top, potatoes, stewed tomatoes, all together on one small plate! Runny mashed bananas and prunes are the dessert. I can eat nothing but part of the dessert. The other food tastes like a mixture of rotten meat and moldy vegetables. Price picks at his plate and eats something. I cannot watch him put such horror into his mouth. In the cabin we have some peanut butter and crackers we brought along to munch on.

Bed is soft and sinking, and I plunge into it, heavy-eyed with sleep, not planning to dream of baboons. We have to be up very early to ride in an open truck over the reserve.

"Do you think we'll see any elephants?" I query Price, trying to enclose myself in netting draped voluminously from a point in the ceiling to all sides of the bed. On the opposite side of the room, Price is having trouble, getting entangled with the netting over his bed.

"Think I'm going to sleep without this thing around the bed," he mumbles.

"You'd better not. Remember you may be eaten up by mosquitoes!" I warn him.

I get out of my bed and help him adjust the yards and yards of soft white net material. He resembles a bride with bridal veils around him. We laugh and laugh at the effect. Finally we turn out the lights.

Price remembers my question and calls out, "Whoever sees the first elephant tomorrow gets a prize."

Saturday, April 8th

Our alarm clock rings. We dress and drink coffee brought by a man from the restaurant. I look at the rickety open-bed truck we are to ride in and wonder where we will sit. It looks fit only for cattle. Twelve of us step up and into the truck, standing and holding onto the wooden slatted sides. We start down a dusty wide path through a forest, then skirt a swampy area clear of trees but heavy with muck and vegetation. We are to be gone all morning, and there are no seats for anyone! Later I discover I am so excited I could not have stayed seated anyway.

We pass tracks made by elephants in the mud around a watering hole. Our guide says they have been there only recently because there is fresh elephant dung to be seen. We strain our eyes looking as far as possible. We see a large ugly wart hog, facing us, in a clump of brush. How strangely exciting this is to see a wild animal in its natural environment. I find myself exclaiming "oh" and "oh look." Around a curve we come upon a family group of some fifty or more baboons scattered in trees, making chattering noises and eating. We ride slowly past them. Near a pile of large rocks sits a mother baboon with her tiny baby clinging to her. An old gray grandfather baboon lounges nearby.

Farther down the narrow road, our guide points to a water buffalo lying down, stuck in a mud hole. Away to the left of the hole, watching from brown bush grass is a herd of seven water buffalo with heads up. The guide says the stuck buffalo will die there. We pass two different herds of bush bucks, lying near trees as brown as they are. It is incredible how these animals are well camouflaged by the natural world around them. We fail to sight any elephants or duikers (antelopes) or lions.

Around a curve in the road a black and green iridescent-hued heron stands in the murky swamp water along with an enormous black stork wearing a white ring around its neck. Here our truck driver stops for us to make pictures. Otherwise, we aim our camera while bumping and swerving along in the truck. We begin to see fallen trees and trees stripped of bark where elephants graze and eat.

Our guide speaks only a smattering of English. All he does is point to the animals and call them by English names. We need a more knowledgeable guide. Even so, the sights are thrilling. We pass a better watering place, the water green and clear where water lilies float in the middle. No birds or animals here.

The narrow, dirt-packed road begins to wind through stretches where fires have burned trees. Soon the truck driver moves toward rocky, dry ground thick with scrubby green bushes and palm trees. How quickly the land changes here from one variety of typography to the next. Here green jungle-like vines hang overhead in tree tops. Fiery-colored birds, blue and red with orange-circled necks, green, orange, and deep green flash in and out among the trees. Our truck driver begins to turn back toward the huts and restaurant. I want to stay longer looking for animals instead of being with people. I can understand now why men and women go to live among and to study the wild animals.

Price and I go for soap and towels we had brought with us,

then trek to the banks by the warm springs to wash faces and hands. There are no bathtubs or showers in the huts.

At noon we begin the long, hot drive returning to Jos, an endurance test I think will never end. Down we go into one big chuckhole in the road, then into the next one. We drink all the filtered water brought in jugs from Jos. We snack on a few crackers but have nowhere to stop for lunch. I cling by one hand to the strap on my upper right in the back seat. The miles stretch on and on. I keep remembering the happy baboons in the tall baobab trees. In Jos, at last, and too tired to talk.

Sunday, April 9th

We slept last night in Frances Knight's pleasant house near the Jos school where she teaches. What is there about some homes? You walk in and immediately have a sense of well-being, of a place being cared for, of things in order, colors and light that comfort and soothe. As long as we are not going to live outdoors amid the grandeur and loveliness of nature, we have to create our world of beauty indoors where we live. I am grateful for this change of scenery, a real oasis after Yankari.

We are crowded returning to Ogbomosho with the Millers. With us is the fifteen-year-old son of one of the couples living in Ogbomosho, who rides with Price and me in the back seat. I sit up on the edge of the seat over a worn out seat spring. Riding gets more and more uncomfortable.

We pass groves of eucalyptus trees, their sharp, clean scent delicious to smell. Then down again from the high plateau country to bush and villages and Fulani. We see some grain storage bins near one village, looking like fat dwarfs with long thatched-roof hair. In one stretch of road, gutted with holes, an iron pipe falls from underneath the car. We stop briefly. Villagers gather around the car and point and laugh at us. Since no one knows whether we need it or not, we travel on uneasily, taking the pipe in the car.

I try to sleep, suggest singing, anything to help cope with this backbreaking ride. Dust, heat, and unrelenting wind surge through the open windows onto our faces.

Three hours away from Ogbomosho the station wagon's generator burns out and we are stopped, immobile on the highway.

110

It is 4:30 P.M. and nowhere near would there be a garage. Paul Miller hitches a ride with a passing truck driver. The four of us, left to wait, cross a ditch and find slight shade under scrawny trees. Scrubby bush and rocks surround us. We take to the bush for bathroom necessities, then sit on rocks or walk and stand. Eveline Miller sings hymns and reads her Bible. She is confident Paul will find someone who can fix the car. I am not inspired by her words, but suppose I should be. These mission people have learned anything can happen and all must be borne with faith and patience. Suffering and difficulties teach this to some, but I believe one must live years in these circumstances to acquire such stoicism. For them to survive here, this is the only way.

We wait four hours by the side of the highway. The sky lowers toward darkness. Suddenly Miller appears in a car, bringing a sixteen-year-old Nigerian, an apprentice mechanic. I wonder if he is too inexperienced to fix trouble like this car has developed. He works fifteen or so minutes, and the motor turns to running, a good sound. We build a small fire of gathered sticks on the road near the car so trucks will not hit us, now that it is dark. The mechanic lifts his head from the engine of the car and grins. Wonder of wonders!

We go on the road again. I am totally exhausted and frightened to be on the highway at night. No one slows down because of the darkness. Trucks and cars roar past us and toward us going 80 to 90 miles an hour. Singing and joking do not help. I cannot control my emotional state. I begin to cry and want out of the car. We were due in Ogbomosho four hours ago. We have had nothing to eat, and there is nowhere to stop for food. I must stay in this nightmarish situation until we reach Ogbomosho. Miller drives faster and faster. Gasoline trucks and cattle trucks fill the highway. We go lunging through dirt roads under construction, dust flying, around curves passing lorries filled with people and baggage. We are all mad machines flying through the night. Price holds me close in his arms and keeps me becalmed. At last 10:30 P.M. and we pass through the entrance into the seminary campus. "Thank you Lord," I say inwardly again and again.

Monday, April 10th

Wake up in our own bed in Ogbomosho. All morning I think of our three children so far away. I realize afresh what a hardship

111

this must be for mission parents whose children leave for colleges and universities in the States, not the place they call home. And how, as I am doing now, parents left behind anywhere must believe God loves and cares for their children as much as they do. What one does is trust and leave one's children in God's care. We are all there every day, if we are believers. Today I am upheld by a mystery I cannot see or touch, yet I deeply feel the power of God's spirit. Why can one not remain in this state? Why does doubt slip in on some days? Why did my faith not uphold me on the ride last night, when instead I was frantic with fear? Yet I truly believe that when I recover my faith, it is stronger because I go through periods of doubt. Then I pray ever more earnestly for light and guidance and assurance.

This week I am giving the women in English class a vacation. They need time off, as well as I. When I react as I did in the car last night, I need time for rethinking my faith. Human beings can push themselves until they are exhausted. A machine breaks down, yet we try to outdo machines.

Sleep long into the afternoon, awakening when the teakwood trees stand in shadow, not in full sun. Feel joyously better and write letters.

Tuesday April 11th

More rested this A.M., but my legs are still wobbly. Brought on from riding too long in a cramped position in that station wagon. At 5:25 A.M., murky gray dawn outside. Strange how the sunrise is dull and lackluster here. Sometimes I look out the window, at break of day, toward the horizon, watching for pink and rosy hues banded in purple to spread across the sky. I miss wondrous sunrises heralding a new day every now and then.

Went for a walk late in the afternoon with Martha and Alice, both full of energy after working a long day. We walk into the forest a long way back of Frances Jones house. An elderly hunter comes toward us down a path where we walk. He has a gun and a hunter's horn at his side. Martha greets him in Yoruba, and they exchange a few words. She says he lives somewhere in this forest. Farther on we come to a thatched roof round hut where a family lives. No one is there except for several tethered goats. Both Martha and Alice have a great sense of humor, so we laugh

112

as we talk and walk in this almost primeval wood. Martha pretends to see a snake and has me jumping and squealing. I will not soon forget being here on this April afternoon sharing good fellowship in a place untouched by modern civilization.

Wednesday, April 12th

Morning and no class. I hope the women are enjoying this week's vacation as much as I am. They sorely need a rest. I take time at daybreak thinking long thoughts of what is man's purpose on earth, why we are here, and where we are going. I do believe God has a purpose for each life. We are not aimlessly wandering on our pilgrimage through life. We have God as our guide and we find our way through prayer and listening to the Holy Spirit directing us. This does not mean everything will go smoothly or as we would prefer. For me, this means in happy times and suffering times I should give thanks to God. Either my heart should respond, "thank you, God" or cry out, "Lord, my heart fails today, have mercy on me, and grant me peace."

I have learned much about myself in these months. The fear of the unknown still lingers in my psyche somewhere, but not as powerfully. I can survive hardships; I have prayed more and felt closer to God without things getting in the way. I have found more peace living simply and wish this could remain so.

For the first time in my life, I have lived among a community of people who are truly unselfish, thinking of others first, who do not have or do not want a wealth of material goods. Wherever I have lived before, I have never witnessed such dependence on God as an uncomplicated trust. I believe it must be impossible to be unaffected by desire for more whenever people live surrounded by television, advertising, stores bulging with goods, and enough money to buy.

Price is to preach for the Head of State (what he is called here, instead of President or Prime Minister) on Sunday. He will ride from here to Lagos, the capitol city, with Solomon Abegunde, chaplain to the military head of state, Olusegun Obasanjo. Obasanjo lives behind the protected walls of military barracks. He is a Baptist and has his own chapel within the buildings where he lives.

I have decided to remain in Ogbomosho. Martha insists I come

113

to Frances Jones for overnight instead of staying alone in our house. With this week of resting, I hope to be prepared mentally and emotionally for our long trip east to Benin City and Eku.

Thursday, April 13th

The day breaks clear and bright outside the window where I sit. Golden moments though the sky is turning silvery white. Times of silence to be treasured. The world is a lovely place. It is the only world we have.

Here I am able to listen to life, and to observe closely men and women in their frailty, their humility, and oh, especially their tenacity. For endurance is the very backbone of the African character. These people can live through hardships we in the West cannot imagine.

The tremendous concept of the importance of family and the extended family closeness among the Africans impresses me as the core of what sustains them through all the "downs" of their lives. While Nigeria, and all of Africa, needs more technological know-how and advancement, once such modernization transforms their country and their lives, I believe the family may break down as it has done in the West. It is a dilemma. I can see the great need for bettering their lives in so many ways. Yet how I admire and envy their respect for the elderly, their love and communion with children, their regard for the extended family of brothers and sisters as I see this practiced in Ogbomosho, and their ability to enjoy life without artificial stimulation. We in the States are almost unable to enjoy anything that does not unnaturally arouse our senses.

The fresh, fine air of early day is warming. I see the white tunicked Moses, with his hoe slung over his right shoulder, coming down the path toward the garden. He comes earlier this week for some reason. The fruit bat gives one last clanging call. Softly I say farewell to another dawn.

Friday, April 14th

I miss seeing birds when I look out the windows toward the trees and ground. Heat and dry land with no water around must keep them from the area. We did see the brilliant-colored bird in

114

the forest at Yankari. That was farther north. No cats here, only a few mangy dogs, and black and white goats.

Muggy weather this A.M., like August in South Carolina, so different from yesterday. I feel low in energy. To combat this feeling I head for the bedrooms, tidying up, then attack the kitchen. Getting things in order somehow clears my mind. I believe this is an inherited trait. My mother liked and kept a lovely, shining house.

There is a rich, yellow light this noon on the bronze and gold plants that hedge the house where we live. Moses waters them almost daily, carrying buckets of water to splash and cool their leaves. I can look out the windows through these high plants at the back toward the garden. Two bananas hang on a leafy plant near the windows. Slowly they are turning pale yellow.

Price and I walk late in the afternoon when the sun hides behind clouds for a change. We walk for the needed exercise, trying not to be bothered by the dust kicked up by our feet or the sweat on our brows.

Saturday, April 15th

Rain and wind in the night and again at 3:00 A.M. Price slept on soundly. I was up shutting the glass-louver windows in the living room and in our bedroom. Breezes are so cool and delightful I want to run outdoors and feel the rain on my face, wind in my hair. I slept finally under a top sheet for the first time since January!

At breakfast we talk about what we are going to eat. We have had peanut butter and banana sandwiches for lunch for three days and beans for two days. Weeks ago, I found a jar of peanut butter on a shelf in the pantry. The woman whose house we occupy while she is in the States left it. We make good use of this staple since there is none in local stores. Price's trader woman left us seven bruised tomatoes on the back steps yesterday.

Rain falls slowly and gently, collecting in drops on the clothesline outside. Price leaves, walking under an umbrella, to go teach his classes. The house is cozy and quiet while water runs off the roof and splashes on the earth. I read an old copy of *Time* magazine, then do needlepoint. While I draw the needle in and out, I think about the missionaries teaching and working on this mission field. It is difficult to face the reality of life here. Mission people react in different ways to avoid dealing with reality, even as people do everywhere in the States.

One way is to be a Pollyanna and always say everything turns out for the best or will do so. Another way is to be "on stage" and focus attention on who you are or what you are doing. Or some flee reality by withdrawing and becoming reclusive. Generally though, at this seminary, there are only a few who fall into any of these traps. I find it interesting to observe what people anywhere do or become rather than be real or authentic.

Sunday, April 16th

Price is leaving at 7:00 A.M. to drive with Solomon Abegunde to Lagos. At 5:30 A.M. we are up, eating cereal and drinking coffee. A heavy, misty fog shrouds the trees, bushes, everything outdoors. Fortunately, Abegunde is an hour late. By the time they are in the car to go, visibility is better. I am thankful they will not be on the highway in fog.

Gardenias are blooming on a bush near the window where I iron curtains and clothes. Finally, the enveloping mist lifts, and the air is exceedingly warm. Gloria comes to the back door. No water at the married students' dorm, she reports. When she leaves, we fill a large bucket with water. Gloria deposits it expertly on top of her head and walks toward the dorm. I give her some gardenias to take along, also. There must be something of beauty for Gloria this day.

Late in the afternoon, I walk to Frances Jones. Martha insists I come to spend the night.

I return to our house for sleeping things, then back to eat supper by candlelight with a small group on the front screened porch. I sleep in a large room, opening onto a wide veranda on both sides. Martha has a vacuum of coffee for me to take to the bedroom in case I awake before breakfast. I open both long windows to the cooler night air. I sleep fitfully hearing a clock in the hall strike midnight, then four. After that, I toss, turn, flip on a light, read the Bible and a book about Switzerland Martha gave me last night. The coffee is hot and imbues me with a cheerful feeling, alone in this strange bed in the dark morning. After an hour, I am down in the bed again, lights out, going to sleep to the sound of the clock ticking, a pleasing sound of comfort.

Monday, April 17th

I awaken to a lovely morning. I try to be quiet because Martha had to go to the hospital last night when the gardener at Frances Jones came rushing in with his child almost dead from dehydration.

The boy's mother gave him a dose of locally concocted medicine. Early this morning Martha left again for the hospital to treat Matthew's child, Ambrose. He had a stiff neck and fever. Yesterday morning she hurried to the hospital to help with an emergency Caesarean section, the fifth one for a Nigerian woman, and awhile later did a hysterectomy on another woman. Martha has strength and courage. How I do admire her!

Late in the morning, after Martha returns, we have breakfast on the porch. We look out toward the huge scarlet blossoms of the flame trees in the yard and toward the bluish-shaded hills in the far distance. Matthew has the table set with a white cloth and a centerpiece of snowy white lilies. He is smiling now because Martha assures him that Ambrose will be better soon. Lech comes to join us and tells about his home in Poland, near a forest. He is happy this morning recalling his homeland and the Polish peoples' love of flowers and fruit.

"We always have flowers in the house," Lech recalls "if only a few." So far away from home and family and all he loves, this good and decent man needed to share his thoughts with us. So it was that the three of us had a meeting of mind and spirit—one of those privileged times of relationships.

I walk back to our house refreshed. I miss Price deeply today. With him away from my side, I feel alone in a strange land. When he is with me, anywhere we are together is our home.

Tuesday, April 18th

Went to Antioch church last night for a special service. Sitting there, looking out the open window, I tried to fix forever in my mind the sight of flowering flame trees and tall palms outlined against the darkening night sky. Small boys outside were kicking a ball in an empty field, and down the dirt road, parallel to the church, a tall man walked, his long, white tunic robe billowing in the breeze. Like someone trying to memorize a speech, I study the earnest faces of students sitting around me in church. I wish that I could remember every individual face but know that is impossible.

I stay the night again at Frances Jones. Martha tells me about her early days in Ogbomosho, before her husband died. She hated the place and the land at first but felt so strongly that her place was in Africa. I marvel at her courage through all these years. After breakfast, I return to our house. Price arrives late in the afternoon and has had a great time in Lagos. He spoke to a student assembly at a school near the church, as well as for the Head of State. He and the chaplain rode on a new expressway from Ibadan to Lagos, with light traffic. This was because the chaplain was allowed access to a highway not yet open to the public.

Wednesday, April 19th

This morning in chapel an extraordinary thing happened. Another student named David was the speaker. He proceeded to lay it on the faculty for not being more spiritual and for emphasizing the academic side of life too much. He talked about the faculty not giving students opportunities to have open discussions and for making their homes off limits to the students. David said the faculty should visit the student residences and show more concern for them. He was almost shouting in an angry voice. It was not the place or the time to be speaking on such thoughts, or maybe it was. David is young and brash and courageous, but did not use good judgment. I am sure he will be reprimanded soundly by the administration.

I felt a heavy sadness for him. It must be terribly difficult to see the Americans living in houses with luxuries these students do not have. A real dilemma exists here. Housing for students is substandard compared with American-style dormitories. Yet for them, these small rooms in a building with concrete floors and walls is better than where they once lived in mud houses or thatch-roofed huts with earthen floors.

Missionaries have their own furniture shipped from the US by the Foreign Mission Board. The interiors of their houses look luxurious compared to the students' rooms. Since the students do not like Western food, to entertain them socially is difficult. In a way, a social barrier does exist between the students' residences and the faculty homes.

No bread is available in the Ibadan supermarket this week. Marjorie has Sam, the cook at Frances Jones, bake us a loaf. I look longingly at Moses' garden, hoping the vegetables will hurry and mature.

Thursday, April 20th

Return to English class this morning after a weeks absence. The women seem more alert and less tired. I hope the vacation was a time of relaxation for them. It was for me. At break time, I find a letter from our sons. The two of them have enjoyed a wonderful week together skiing in the Colorado mountains. Since Douglas lives in Wisconsin and Philip in North Carolina, their times of get-together are rare.

In the afternoon, Leslie Williams comes to talk about the long trip we will make with her and a driver, Mr. Udo, to Benin City and to Eku. We will ride in an air conditioned Land Rover because of taking medical supplies to the hospital in Eku. Again we will need to provide our own supply of food and water. Leslie says on this journey we will drive on some stretches of better paved roads. To my delight, she reports that there may be a chance for us to go swimming in a river near Eku! What a treat that would be!

The men in class tonight get into an argument over the interpretation of scripture passages on which they had been give a writing assignment. All of them talk in loud and spirited voices. All, except Stephen, the gentle soul in this class, who speaks always quietly and slowly. He listens, meditates, and tells one student who is vociferous to be more calm. These are grown men and I am amazed at how anger seems to flare so quickly, yet I have been told that the Nigerians love to argue as much as they love to sing.

In fact, it is said that the people here worry the least, sing the most, argue the loudest, fall asleep the fastest, and are the friendliest of anywhere in Africa. Certainly they seem to take great joy in bickering over prices in the marketplaces and I see them fall asleep anywhere and everywhere. And even though their daily diet holds little variety, they get immense satisfaction from eating. All in all life for them is noisy, colorful, and punctuated with humorous gaiety.

119

In a place where the unexpected is always happening, why should I be surprised at this climate in the classroom? The electricity witnessed this evening is much better than dull, apathetic students.

We pack our clothes for our trip early in the morning. I boil eggs, make cheese sandwiches, and fill a thermos with water before bedtime. All this will need to last the first long day to Benin City.

Friday, April 21st

Neither of us slept well. Price says he did not sleep after 1:00 A.M. I was kept awake by his tossing and turning in the bed. Mrs. Imasogie's hens cackled loudly for a long time. Mrs. Imasogie, the vice principal's wife, is an interesting Nigerian lady. She has an M.A degree in seventeenth century English from an American college and she raises chickens. Her hen house is in back of the Imasogie's house beside the path we walk from our place to Frances Jones. Very near. When the wind is from certain direction, we often get a strong chicken house smell blowing our way.

Late in the morning, we load our things into the Land Rover and leave with Leslie Williams and Mr. Udo, the Nigerian driver He knows only a smattering of English, so he and Leslie speak a local language together. How wonderful is the air-conditioned car. No hot wind whipping your face. I sit back in my seat and relax, even though the first of our trip is over the gutted road to Oshogbo.

We go on another road worse than the first one—more holes, cracks, and deep ruts in the dry earth. Suddenly we meet a car and the driver waves at us to stop. He tells us that Nigerian students are rioting at the University of Ife, rioting because the government has decided to charge a fee for food costs instead of free meals. He warns us to change our route and not pass by Ife. A professor has been beaten badly.

Mr. Udo decides to use another better but longer road. Jungle vegetation grows heavier and heavier on either side of this road. We begin to see greater concentrations of palm and rubber trees. Along the roadside in many places, Nigerians are selling plantain and the largest pineapples I have ever seen. Some look a foot or more long. Leslie says pineapples from this area are the best in Nigeria. Nearly thirty miles from Benin City, we come onto a paved four-lane highway. Wonder of wonders, like nothing I've seen in this country before. Mr. Udo drives faster and faster. Toward dark we enter the outskirts of the city. It resembles entering Ogbomosho—small stores, people everywhere, walking the road, milling about, going in stores, standing and watching everybody else. Cars, noise, and confusion.

We find the gate that leads to the driveway toward Mildred Crabtree's house, where we are to spend this night and the following day and night. Mildred, a student worker at University of Benin, has a comfortable place and gives us supper, ending with delicious pineapple slices. We are tired and sleepy by 8:00 P.M. A gusty wind is rising outside, cooling the dark and sultry air blowing through open windows. We go to bed to the sound of rain beating in a steady noise on the tin roof of the house. I know the rain will not cool the air for long because we are nearer the equator now. Since arriving in the house, the heat has been like a wool blanket over my head the middle of a summer day. I am not hungry for food, only for relief from the heat. I lie in bed, my neck collecting beads of sweat against the pillow, knowing it will be a long night.

Saturday, April 22nd

I am awake at 4:00 A.M., lying still, and gazing toward the window past the clock on the bedside table. The world outside is dark and silent. It is as always with me—the first night in a strange place I cannot sleep.

Today, Price and I go with Mildred and Leslie to tour Benin City. Benin was a powerful state at the height of its power in the fifteenth and sixteenth centuries. It remained secure and contained until 1877, when it ran afoul of the British. The British attempted to impose protection and enforce abolition of slavery and sacrifice to gods. The British Acting Consul General insisted on seeing the *Oba*, or king, during a religious festival when the *Oba* was not to lay eyes on a stranger. The Acting Consul was killed, along with five other British officials.

The British retaliated by burning down Benin City, capturing the *Oba*, and carrying off 2,500 of the most valuable bronzes to the museums of Europe. The fifteenth century *Oba*'s palace is in the town center, surrounded by high walls, and is not open to the public. The seventeenth century Dutch geographer, Olfert Dapper, described the palace as having "wooden pillars encased in copper where their victories are depicted."

In the city, we visit a large church, with fifteen-feet-high hand-carved, ebony doors. They are breathtaking to behold, the wood dark and satiny to feel, solid wood with intricately carved Biblical scenes from top to bottom of each door. Such majestic doors attached to an otherwise plain building on a muddy street. I hope the people who worship here take notice of this skilled craftsmanship.

In the main part of the city, we have to drive around a circle, called a roundabout, to get to the street of the museum we are hunting. Here we enter to view the famous Benin bronzes—carved statuary produced between the sixteenth and nineteenth centuries. These bronzes are the most famous of all Nigerian sculpture, as well as the oldest and most beautiful. Bronze, ivory, and wood sculptures were used in the *Oba*'s court for many hundreds of years. Artists belonged to guilds under the protection of the *Oba*. Human and animal figures were carved. Most Nigerian bronzes were produced by the lost-wax process. A model of wax or latex was sandwiched between two layers of sun-baked clay, held in place with iron pins. The wax or latex was melted out and replaced by molten bronze.

In this museum, ebony sculptured heads glow as though freshly rubbed with palm oil. A bronze rider on horseback, carved in the eighteenth century, is my favorite and rivals one of Rodin's bronzes.

Mildred takes me to a small, hole-in-the-wall shop where hand carving of wood is done by two expert craftsmen, not mass produced. The first piece I spy is a finely carved head of a young Fulani girl, carved from King Ebony wood and smooth as polished marble. Her hair is pulled tight on each side of her head and hangs in minutely carved braided pigtails, exactly like I have seen on the Fulani women in bush country. The carving speaks to me; I know it will do so forever. Mildred buys a King Ebony mask that I admired.

Russell Locke, a missionary from around the Owerri area, arrives and soon leaves, taking Price with him for a trip into more remote country. I am to go alone with Mr. Udo, our driver on a two-hour drive to Eku and spend the night with the John McFaddens, who are expecting me. Later, Mr. Udo will drive to Owerri to bring Price back to Eku. From there we will return to

Benin City for Leslie; then, after an overnight, begin the journey back to Ogbomosho. I chose not to go to Owerri because of being on the road a longer time. In Eku I will try and rest while waiting for Price.

Eku is in the Delta country, Niger River country, lowlands. Mid-afternoon, hot and steamy outside, and I get in the Land Rover with Mr. Udo driving, while I ride beside him in the front seat. I say good-bye to Mildred and Leslie.

We leave the city in the midst of heavy traffic and congestion, horns honking, people running in front of cars, lorries loaded with passengers and luggage on top. At last we reach a flat and better road, where here and there are stands with stacked pineapples for sale. Mr. Udo is an excellent driver; he never takes an unnecessary chance.

Soon we are in Sapele, a town looking like others in Nigeria. Cars are lined up for a mile to buy petrol at a filling station. We turn into a narrow road, full of deep holes, cracked macadam, ragged edges, dirt paths along the sides. Some jolts send me off the seat and I bounce down, gritting my teeth. Long past Sapele, looking out the window, I see we are traveling mile after mile by gray-barked trees—dense forests that darken the light on the road. Our car is alone on the road. Mr. Udo and I are the only persons riding through this mysterious-looking gloomy land.

"What kind of trees are those, Mr. Udo?" It is the first time I speak since leaving Benin City. I want him to concentrate on driving. Besides, it suits me fine not to talk. "Rubber," was Mr. Udo's brief answer. I am surprised he understood my question.

Suddenly he stops the car. He says nothing, gets out and disappears. I sit alone in the car, my heart racing, wondering what Mr. Udo might be up to. I think to myself, "what in the world am I doing here on a road with a strange man deep in a rubber forest in Africa?" It is a question that keeps me laughing inwardly for the remainder of the trip, after Mr. Udo reappears. He climbs into the car and without a word we proceed on our journey. I assume Mr. Udo had to find a place to relieve himself.

Further on, we begin to pass signs like "Medicine Man" or "Ju Ju Man" in front of small houses. Many such notices in front houses. One humorous sign (to me) read, "Healing House, Herb Doctors for Swollen Persons." The countryside flattens and reminds me of land in South Carolina nearing the coastline. I know that in this part of Nigeria, ancient religious rites continue to be practiced. The sky deepens from dirty gray to dark twilight. I feel uneasy and tired. I ask Mr. Udo to drive faster so we can be in Eku by dark. He speeds up, but I wonder how he feels about my asking him to do that. He does not talk. I see a sign, "5 miles to Eku," and am thankful.

Sunday, April 23rd

Last night the John McFaddens welcomed me to their house in Eku on the compound near the hospital where McFadden is a doctor. Houses and hospital buildings are set among palm trees flowering shrubs, banana trees, and pineapple bushes. We ate fried fresh fish for our evening meal. Weariness finally crept up my body like a slow fever. I sank into bed under a whirring ceiling fan, thankful to be where I could sleep and not think.

Today I go to another doctor's house for lunch. Gazing around the living room, I notice books I would like to read. But the doctor's wife wants to talk. Those who live and work here are lonely. Eku is a more remote place than is Ogbomosho and fewer Americans are around for visits. I sense her great need to see other faces and to communicate. So we talk. Late in the afternoon I nap.

I think of Price and Mr. Udo on the road coming through the jungle from Owerri. It is 5:00 P.M. by my watch. The doctor is playing a record again, this one of someone singing hymns in a loud voice. I wait through supper with the doctor and his wife for a car to turn into the driveway, scarcely wanting any food. By 6:00 P.M. a pit of inky darkness surrounds the house. I pace back and forth across the living room to the kitchen door, gazing toward the road for a sign of car lights. At 7:00 P.M., Price and Mr. Udo arrive after a delay of two hours, due to traffic backed up at a wreck on the highway. Every time mission people drive on highways in Nigeria, their families and friends know the possibility of their death is very real.

I go to bed thinking how strange and wonderful this world is and life in it. Yet in the end one's work is within one's own heart. Only God enters there.

"The keys to the heart . . .

. . . are at the cincture hung of God;

Its gates are trepidant to His nod;
By Him its floors are trod."
—Francis Thompson

Monday, April 24th

Early in the morning I awake and sit on the side of the bed, looking out the window. Morning is overcast and rainy, but the view of a forest, thick and dark with trees, is lovely. Past the palm trees and the rubber trees is a swamp, then the river. Hibiscus hedges arrayed in red blossoms and flowering, orange-red flame trees dot the lawn. All the vegetation has a luscious, sensuous look that makes me exuberant.

Price talks excitedly about his trip to Owerri. He was deep in native country, once part of Biafra, where during the Civil War in Nigeria, the federal forces starved out the Ibo people. He was taken to see indigenous shrines far into the jungle. I wish now that I had gone with him, but we are to go later to Oshogbo to see similar sights.

Once there was a large rubber industry flourishing in Eku. Since oil was discovered near and off the coast of Nigeria, more money is made working on the oil rigs; consequently, the rubber industry has lost ground. Last night I was shown the spiral red flares of fire fanned out by oil rigs located on the river rigs, many miles from Eku. Like a beautiful sunset, the red glow lighted up the countryside beyond the town.

We go to church for a special service. Men wearing long skirts, shirts, straw hats, and carrying cane sticks, and women in the long, tightly-wrapped, flowered skirts, blouses, and geles fill the seats. Children run in and out the open church doors. The language here is mainly Urhobo. The speaker tells them to be quiet. One woman lays her baby on the floor by the communion table. A small girl sitting by me eats pieces of dry bread from her purse. Drums and bell clappers are the only instruments to accompany our singing. As we leave the building a group of men, women, and children walk toward us swaying, clapping, and singing. It is their way of telling us we are welcome and of saying good-bye.

We have an abundant dinner at the McFaddens'. I am so hungry for this Western-type food that I quickly overeat. Someone wants to know if Price and I would like to go swimming in the Ethiope

125

River ten minutes up the road. We readily answer yes. We are delighted to find a clear body of water, clean and pale green with heavy jungle on the opposite side from where we swim. Wild white flowers bloom among the trees. Price and I jump into the river from an old diving board and yell back and forth to each other like children at play. The water moves with a strong current but is refreshingly cold and pure. It is a perfect time to relax because in several hours we are to start the long trek back to Benin City with Mr. Udo.

We are on the road by mid-afternoon, having to detour because of a washed-out road. We buy five large pineapples from a roadside stand. Their ripe scent perfumes the car. Finally into Benin City, we are tired, ready for rest, but we are invited to eat with a newly-arrived mission couple at a house near the University of Benin. Again we are needed to talk with people lonely to visit people of their own kind. Loneliness is a hard reality mission personnel must live with daily. Yet I think of lonely people in our own country. Is not loneliness a state of the mind?

When we return to Mildred Crabtree's house, in the evening light we can see a procession of men and women dancing down the street. Someone is beating a drum, and a huge wooden-carved figure, covered in cloth with mirrors shimmering at its stomach, is being held aloft and conveyed by two men. Mildred says these are worshipers carrying their idol and going to some place for a sacrifice. The sight is ominous and gruesome because of the earnestness of people caught up in emotional fervor.

Tuesday, April 25th

Back in the Land Rover this morning and on our way to Ogbomosho. We are on a smooth macadam road for a brief time. We stop and again buy pineapple; one weighs fifteen pounds. I think about the high cost of pineapples in Hawaii. These Nigerian pineapples are the best I have ever eaten.

We turn off the highway onto a narrow road bordered on each side by dense, short palm growths and cocoa plants. We pass small thatch-roofed villages where old men idly sit outside under the shade of trees, watching with squinted eyes. The women are busy selling pineapples or red hot peppers or carrying buckets on their heads down a path leading into the undergrowth.

A cobalt blue sky, where puffy white clouds float, brightens the day like the breathtaking sight of the sky on a clear October day in the Carolina mountains. We ride in silence, each of us seemingly affected by the beauty of the heavens and the quieter road to travel. Life is too rich to waste; it is more than mere existence. The Roman philosopher, Seneca, thought that the part of life we live is often too small and we should really live each day fully. I am grateful for the time to be in this country and among these Nigerians where I can show friendship and kindness and share in their worth as human beings and in the eyes of God. The fact that we have come a long way to be their friends seems to mean much to many of them.

On we go, eating peanut butter sandwiches and bananas, back over holes in the road to Iwo. After Iwo and Oyo, we near Ogbomosho. By now seeing this place is like coming home.

Wednesday, April 26th

A day beginning like so many others here, watching for daybreak, thinking, and loving the quietness. I sit alone in the dark living room, without a candle lighted. Looking out the window into darkness, I see no familiar outline of trees or bushes. Nothing but darkness, yet I know assuredly that light will break soon. Alone, I wait, in a strangely unfriendly room. In the dark I see no comforting familiarity of possessions. Here I am existing alone with no one to pose for, to hear my ideas, or with whom to be intimate. Can I stand myself or shall I escape into daydreaming or sleep or eat or find fellow company? In a way this is scary. Yet I know I can depend on the coming of dawn, a sign of God's presence in the world, and so I can rest contented.

I find solitude and silence necessary for well-being. Yes, some part of the day for me needs to be spent in quietness, allowing me to collect myself. Years spent actively rushing from here to there when our children were young, before I began teaching, and Price was a seminary professor, then pastor of a busy metropolitan church, are over. Now there is time to deal with my own soul's longings, to read more, to talk about things that matter, and to learn more about who I am and where I am in life's great journey. A sad fact to me is that many persons growing older seem to increase their activity in a non-stop round of mindless going and coming, in order not to be bored.

I walk the narrow dirt path going to English class. No longer am I wary of a snake or rat coming from the bushes as the path turns into a wider road. How soon once unknown places can become familiar. When I return to the house, a stranger is in the back yard washing clothes in our laundry tubs and hanging them on our lines. I say nothing to him. Nigerians tend to believe everything is community property. Perhaps Nat told him to use these facilities.

In the afternoon, Price takes a long nap and feels more rested, he says. The heat begins to take its toll unless you slow down. For Americans, the habit of overdoing is soon tempered to a routine of work and rest here.

We both are weary from our long trip to Benin City and decide on a long night's sleep. The watchman comes to sit on the porch, and we give him an orange and a banana to eat. Tall and gaunt, his leathered face and unfathomable eyes remind me of some well-carved Nigerian mask. We are like passengers on different ships passing each other in the night, no way to know each other.

Thursday, April 27th

When the rooster in Mrs. Imasogie's chicken yard next door starts crowing and the fruit bat stops its strange calling, I know daylight is nearing. I am up and open the back door. A blackish green frog sits on the porch staring back at me, the first frog I have seen in Nigeria. Poor thing. He will not long survive there when the orange and gray lizards appear.

After breakfast, Gloria comes to clean the house. She soon reports that her husband has chicken pox, catching it from one of their children. She says he has been in bed two days and is very sick. I tell her Price and I will visit him later in the day. Gloria is frightened by what is happening to David, I can tell. I try to reassure her that he will recover, even though he may look terrible now.

When Price returns to the house, we put mangoes, pawpaws, oranges, bread, and tea bags in a sack and walk to the married students' dorm. We want Gloria to have the fruit and tea for David and to leave some money they will need. All their children have been sick with the pox, evidently.

There are no screens on the windows in their small three-room quarters for five people. David is lying on a bed in a mini-size room, and one of the children is asleep on a bed in a similar room.

128

Flies crawl on the bed. His face, neck, and arms are covered with white ointment. His bloodshot eyes show all the misery he feels. He looks terrible but says he is happy his throat has opened so he can sing and praise God. Gloria and David express the thought that the devil is working against them in order to tempt them. We stay only briefly, leaving the food and tea bags, and expressing words of sympathy. Then we stand around the bed, in the suffocating heat of the room, while Price prays a short prayer for them. When we leave, both of us walk in silence down the dirt path shadowed by teak trees. I am overcome with emotion, part anger and part sadness. I am holding back tears in my eyes. When I look at Price, so is he.

Why do these people have to live like that when we and the other foreigners here live like we do? If we gave up all our possessions, how many families would that help? Probably only a few for a brief time. The problem is mind-boggling.

Friday, April 28th

During the night, I was kept awake by drums incessantly drumming from midnight until early morning. The drumming was going on in two different places, carrying messages back and forth. Loud voices chanting, almost screaming, were mixed in with the drumming. Yesterday, local secondary school students carrying clubs, marched in a demonstration protesting their standards of education. Primary school students were seen throwing their books in dirty puddles of water. I imagine the townspeople are in an uproar and the long, intense drumming is a way of venting their feelings.

We drive in the rain to the mission prayer meeting at the Gaventa's house. Bill rushes in from the hospital and later, in his calm and gentle way, speaks of the story of David and Goliath for our devotional. He says that we all face Goliaths in our lives at one time or another and that we need faith like David's. There are many Goliaths in this land, so much corruption in high places, power-hungry people who could not care less about the poor, and the breakdown daily of necessities for living. Yet the same things occur in the US and all over the world. In Nigeria, chaos is a way of life. Will it become that for Americans, also, someday, I wonder?

Today we are to travel that deep-rutted road to Oshogbo again for the last time. We are to meet the Wilfred Congdons, a couple who came to Nigeria over forty years ago to direct construction of mission buildings. He and his wife retire this year and will return to live in the States. I suppose part of them will always be in Africa, yet, in a sense, Africa will be with them in memory, no matter where they go. No doubt about it, this land has a fascination and a mystery that unsettles you.

Mr. Congdon plans to take us to see several artists' places of work. Oshogbo developed an artists' colony through the years, mainly because of Suzanne Wengel, an Austrian sculptress who came there to live twenty years ago. She married a Nigerian and became a priestess of the cult of Oshun. She encouraged worship of the Goddess Oshun, goddess of the river and of fertility, by creating enlarged, stylized statues and carvings in a sacred grove outside Oshogbo. Apparently, she also brought together the work of artists in wood carving, painting, and batik work. One artist from here had his work in repousse aluminum panels exhibited in the Smithsonian in Washington. Carved on the panels are subjects often based on African folk tales.

When we turn into the driveway of the Congdon's place, I think I am dreaming. A large lawn stretches in front of their house, the grass green and freshly mowed. Pots of dracaena and diffenbachia line the back yard, and flashy pink and red caladiums bloom in front and back. Along with African daisies there are ferns, palm trees, and snowy white flowers. Inside the house everything is polished and shiny clean. What a difference orderliness and cleanliness can make. And to think not ten minutes ago we were passing mud houses set in dirt yards. I stand for a long time inside the house gazing out the front window at the yard and flowers.

Price and I go in the car with Mr. Congdon to places where artists work. We park by a ditch filled with green, slimy water, walk past a Yoruba woman having her hair wound on thread by another woman, and a child shaving a coconut with a razor blade. We turn up a dirty stairway to a room where the intricately carved aluminum panels, depicting Nigerian village life, are piled in corners of the room. We meet no artist there.

From there, we drive to a wild forest area near the Oshun River. We go through a weirdly carved entrance, get out and walk down a narrow path descending toward the river. A Yoruba man suddenly appears out of dense undergrowth to our right. He is shabbily dressed and a long knife hangs at his side from a belt around his waist. We keep walking toward him, while Mr. Congdon greets him in Yoruba. He watches us pass, then disappears among the dense trees. I sense Mr. Congdon thinks we are safe.

We come close to a large hut, the shrine to Oshun, open on all sides, with a dirt floor and used as a worship center. Behind it is the Oshun, a fast-flowing river, framed by the giant trees in the sacred grove. When we walk nearer to the water, I see a twenty-foot-tall figure of a woman, carved in dark wood, standing upright in the water.

This statue represents Oshun, the goddess of fertility. Women who have no children come to this place to pray to Oshun to help them be childbearers. Where we stand, the dark green, lush vegetation, nestled at the base of tall, leafy trees, encloses us in a mysterious twilight. I shiver, not with fright, but with awe that I am trespassing sacred territory. We climb out of this quiet grove to a flat area of land where stand grotesque-appearing figures, cast in clay, as gigantic as reconstructed dinosaur skeletons. Mr. Congdon says these are worshiped in secret ceremonies. From there, we walk a path through woods, dark with close spaced trees and eerily silent, to a tribal ceremonial house. No one is here and probably we are not welcome in this place. On we plunge, however, stooping low to enter a small door of the tomblike, round-shaped construction of mud and thatched roof. There are no windows in the place and wood poles undergird the sloping walls outside.

Inside, the one large room is curved in a semicircle, with places for sitting on the dirt floor, leaning one's back against the wall. We see altar places on the floor containing piles of ashes. Some sort of sacrifice, of course. I dare not look closely for fear I might see something gruesome. We move quickly out of the place and hurry down the path to the car. I have a feeling someone's eyes are watching us within the underbrush wherever we have gone. My heartbeat quickens until we are in the car and on the highway leading into the town some five miles away.

In Oshogbo, there is also a shrine to Obatala, who is widely acknowledged by the Yoruba people to be the most important of the lesser gods. According to Yoruba myth, he played the major roll as Olodumare's chief executive in the creation of the world.

131

Obatala himself had been taught by Olodumare how to mold the human form. So he then began to fashion men and women who were infused with the principle of life by the Supreme Being.

Sunday, April 30th

In spite of yesterday's venture into unknown territory, I slept soundly in the Congdon's peaceful house. Price is taking medicine now for a chest cold. He should stay in bed today but he, as always, is excited over the chance to see and learn about another culture.

We sit down to breakfast at a table Esther Congdon has set with paper place mats depicting tribal markings Nigerian children bear on their faces. In the center of the table is a bowl filled with freshly-cut pink and blue hydrangeas. We eat grapefruit, pawpaw, scrambled eggs, guava jelly, muffins, and drink hot coffee. We want to know about their work through the years in this part of the world. We want them to remember when they first came to Nigeria and what it was like then. The stories they tell would make an interesting book and should be recorded by someone. Over this long period of time, they have been collecting native spears, clothes, drums, footstools, and other things. What a display they would make—fit for a museum, I tell them.

Mr. Congdon goes with us to a museum this morning, a branch museum of the University of Ife. In it is a fantastic collection of masks, old ceremonial clothes, iron and brass sculpture, bark painting, carved ceremonial doorposts, old drums, and batik painting. We go to a second artist's house, located at the end of a muddy road. He has his work in batik and wood carving on sale in Washington DC and New York. The lovely batik cloth is done in wild colors and designs, unmistakably African. We miss so much of importance and beauty by not knowing how to look, or by being put off by outer circumstances or appearances. The name of this artist's place is Twin Seven. Seven because he has seven wives.

When Mofeku comes for us in the afternoon, we say good-bye to the Congdons. I look back as the car turns toward the highway and wave what should have been a salute to this humble, kind, and generous couple.

Monday, May 1st

I look at the calendar this morning and realize we will be leaving Nigeria in twenty more days. I want badly to be home now and not have to wait, wait for the news of the birth of Sara's third child. Instead I tell myself to calm down, walk to the window and pray. Somewhere to the west across land and water is our daughter, waiting also.

This place is the most difficult to convey in words on paper, the reality and complexity of people and country. Surely, no one could come to Africa without being changed. Because it is a place that exceeds your expectations, it often puts you on an emotional high.

Coming back from class I meet David, Gloria's husband. His face is marked with chicken pox scars, but he is smiling and stops to thank me for our help and for our prayers. A grateful, sweet people, these. He praised Gloria for all her support of him, saying, "A man's rise or downfall depends on his wife!" This reminds me of a proverb from the Ibo people: "However famous a man is on the outside, if he is not respected in his own house, he is like a bird with beautiful feathers, wonderful on the outside, but ordinary within."

We part company and I walk on thinking about this man, not long from a native village, who has wisdom.

I look out our front door across the road and see construction beginning on the seminary's new music building, not liking what I see. Nigerian women, lined up in a long file, are carrying large pans, filled with gravel, on their heads. They empty the pans, then return for another load. Several of the women are also carrying babies strapped to their waists and backs. I keep thinking of these women during dinner.

135

Tuesday, May 2nd

Overcast sky this morning. I wake up, go for coffee, thinking it may help my headache. Too much doing needlepoint last night by candlelight after the electricity cut off.

I read a recent copy of *Time* magazine Martha loaned me. The sickness in our society is like a festering sore and grows worse. It seems ministers are no longer powers in the pulpit, many of them caught up in the same struggle for success and succumbing to temptation much as everybody else. Where does one look today for noble leaders in the US? Certainly not in the political arena. I sit long this morning at the window pondering, wanting to return to my homeland, but sad to give up this place so removed from the current scene. Yet I know we must again take up our lives there and live out our days, continuing the struggle to try and do right in the midst of wrong.

Here I have been a teacher and a friend of Nigerian people, learned their ways, loved and respected them and am loved and respected by them. I laugh with their laughter and stand by their bedsides when they are sick. I shall miss this close camaraderie when I return to America where we are integrated in name only. There black and white people live in their segregated places, each in his or her own world. We whites do not know the black community in reality, and we remain polarized from each other as much as ever. Sadly, I do not have one black friend that I know well at home.

Wednesday, May 3rd

I walk to the Women's Building down the path overgrown with fast-growing grass, due to the rainy season. Big mud balls made by insects lie on the ground and on the road. I walk around them to avoid getting a shoe full of mud.

After class Alice and I talk about the futility of getting Nigerian women to use birth control methods. A few women have made use of the diaphragm, but several had to have them removed because of trouble developing. The news spreads quickly, alarming other women.

Price naps because he is teaching a seminar on Christian classics tonight, at the request of the mission group. I write the last story on our African experience for the Greenville News and look over discussion material for writing class tonight. Next time we meet, the men will write their final exam and turn in a summary report. I will miss this lively, witty, and intelligent group of men.

Thursday, May 4th

Nat is here promptly at 7:00 A.M. to begin washing our clothes. I like to watch how methodically he goes about his job, filling the tubs outside, each with the exact amount of water from the hose attached to the house. He uses laundry detergent I buy, but rubs and scrubs everything with his hands, gives them a thorough rinse in the second tub, squeezes and twists with his hands to get them dry. Then he hangs towels together, sheets together, blouses, shirts, all systematically on the clothes line. He empties the tubs, leaves them against the house, places the box of detergent on the back porch, gets on his bicycle and is gone for an hour. Clothes dry quickly in the hot morning sun. He is back to take the clothes down, fold them, again putting clothes together that belong together. When this is done, he leaves them in a neat pile on the old washing machine that stands on the back porch. I understand that being hired to do washing is an honored type of work for men in Nigeria.

I go to English class and try today to teach the women how to write a letter. It is a new and trying experience for them. While Patience writes her letter, I hold Benjamin.

Anna, Thomas' wife, writes a letter addressed to me, thanking me for helping her understand things in English. She concludes with a line that touches me deeply, "I thank you because you respect me." I am very moved by the meaning implied in these words from Anna.

After class, Alice comes in her car, and we drive to the main street in Ogbomosho. We walk on a boardwalk over a ditch to get to one shop. Here are thin cotton towels, washcloths, flashlights, plastic combs, plastic mirrors, and baby clothes. I buy farewell gifts for the women in my class. The heat inside the small store is oppressive. Alice suggests we go to her house and have soft drinks, which she has hoarded for a long time. Orange squash, a local favorite drink, is to be found no more in stores.

We sit in Alice's house under the whirring ceiling fans, feet up on low stools, and luxuriate, drinking the cool soda from the refrigerator. Every sip is delicious. Alice looks weary, weary. She does so much for others continually. She needs rest and relaxation.

Solomon Abegunde, chaplain for Gen. Olesegun Obasanjo, Head of State for Nigeria, eats dinner with us at Frances Jones tonight. He talks of marriage customs in Nigeria. He says the father and mother still choose a wife or husband for their son or daughter. If a son marries someone the parents don't approve, they tell him, "OK, if you do this, then don't bring your troubles to us."

Coming out from the house at dark to walk home, we see a sky filled with a splendid, frosty Milky Way and the miraculous splash of gleaming, twinkling billions and billions of stars as if they have been spilled from a bucket.

Friday, May 5th

I slept restlessly all night. Dreamed but this morning could not remember my dream. Still no word about Sara.

The long days of this first week in May pass slowly. I feel so far away from home and our children. I walk from window to window looking for some lovely dawning of light, and only a smoky blur appears on the horizon.

Today I will go with a group of student wives on an all-day outing, a retreat. We ride in a bus to another part of the mission compound in the countryside. The women are leaving their children at the kindergarten center to be cared for by the teachers. Once on the bus, they begin singing and clapping their hands, making music. How good to see them smiling and happy, free of daily responsibilities for a change. A picnic and a craft workshop is planned this morning, along with talks by Carl and Price.

Suddenly I realize Patience is holding her six-month-old Benjamin. She is so attached to this child she cannot part with him for a day, Marjorie tells me.

I look at the weariness shadowing Patience's face. When we step down from the bus to go into the building where the women will meet, I follow Patience closely and whisper, "Patience, let me keep Benjamin outside while you go inside and work in peace for several hours."

Her face clouds, then brightens. Apparently she cannot believe I am offering to look after her child. She smiles and softly answers, "Yes, Mum, you can."

I find a grassy place under the shade of a massive baobab tree

138

and lay Benjamin there on a blue blanket. I sit on the earth beside him. He kicks his fat legs, squeals, and rolls from his stomach to his back. Or he lies quietly, watching the fluttering leaves in the tree overhead.

Minutes pass into an hour. Once Patience comes outside to check on us and leaves. The air puffs soft and heated against my face. As far as my eyes can see, Benjamin and I are alone. I sit with my back leaning against the old tree, meditating in the wondrous silence. I pray for our Sara and her baby, closing my eyes.

How strange that I sit here in Africa taking care of a baby I'll never see again, once I leave here. I am wanting to know about my own child and grandbaby. Yet this moment with Benjamin has a sweetness that brings its own joy. I am flooded with a sense of peace.

Opening my eyes, I seem surrounded by light like one sees occasionally shining in shafts through tall trees in a forest. Within and without me, I am aware of the certainty of God's Holy Spirit, assuring me Sara and her baby are all right. I have a feeling that in days to come, I will know what this day is all about. I sit for a longer time in quietness, holding Benjamin close to me, then we go inside the building to find Patience. In the bus returning to Ogbomosho, I sing joyfully with the women and clap my hands too.

Saturday, May 6th

The air is cooler this morning after an hour of heavy rain during the night.

Price and I talk at breakfast about how to pack our things for going homeward. A student comes riding up on a motorcycle. I run to the door, thinking he may be bringing a letter or news from Sara that came on the Telex in Ibadan. We left word with our children to send any urgent messages to Ibadan, where there is a two-way Telex communication. No word brought by the student, only a letter from a friend of Price's. I am getting jittery waiting for news about Sara and her baby because her due date passed yesterday.

Later in the morning, Price comes from his office to tell me we must drive to Ibadan to have a museum there check on wood carvings and masks we have bought. The Nigerian government does not allow any antiques to leave this country. Nothing we bought is in the antique category.

Afterwards, we walk to Frances Jones and meet Martha's friends from Ibadan. Martha plays songs on the piano from "Sound of Music." I am suddenly very, very tired and need to go to bed. My weariness is more emotional than physical, I am certain.

Sunday, May 7th

I am preparing in my mind to leave Nigeria and return to the United States. I think of the culture shock we will experience in our own milieu again. I know from past experience that it will take several weeks to adjust. Maybe longer, since living in Nigeria has been a greater contrast, another world.

Sitting in Antioch church this morning, I think how accustomed I have become to worshiping with African people. How strange it will be to sit among all American people again. I will miss the power with which these Nigerians sing; I will miss their expressive faces. I know for a time the singing and praying and preaching that goes on in our churches will seem very unimpassioned and maybe stilted. These African people know how to praise God and make a joyful noise!

We go over our itinerary for travel, first to Geneva, out of Lagos on Swiss Air. Then from Geneva we fly to Madrid, rent a car for a trip to Seville and Cordoba, fly from Madrid to Lisbon, Portugal, and from there to New York. We are urging Marjorie to go with us to Geneva. She plans to leave on a year's furlough the same week we leave. She has never been to Switzerland, and we would like to show her this lovely part of the world where we lived for a year. She needs renewal and rest and what better place than Switzerland? I hope she decides to go with us.

I go to bed thinking surely there will be word from Sara this week. I remember the verse in Romans 12, "Be joyful in hope, patient in troubles, and pray at all times."

Monday, May 8th

Oranges and grapefruit are no longer in season and sanitary bread is difficult to find. We are told there have always been seasons when there are food shortages. Only those who maintain a garden and can freeze or can vegetables are able to have a balanced diet.

140

We decide to ship books we brought with us to Nigeria by ocean freight to the States. We have to leave enough open space so that Nigerian customs officials can see exactly what is in the box. We put everything on the floor and work for several hours, packing books and purchases that will remind us of Nigeria. Alice takes the boxes in her car to the post office from where they will go to the port at Lagos for ocean shipping.

Mail brings no word about Sara. I check back through her letters and reaffirm her delivery date of May 1st. Now it is a week later. All I can think of is that the Telex in Ibadan isn't working due to electrical problems.

Tuesday, May 9th

Birds are singing in the darkness outside, and drums are beating far off somewhere. I will miss the drums talking in the night or early morning hours. Something haunting about hearing this clear, rhythmic sound in the midst of silence.

I go to teach English class but discover we are not meeting because the women have to take an exam in music. I walk to the administration building and go to the faculty lounge for a break. Someone has left a bowl of peanuts on the table. I am so hungry I gobble up a handful.

Still hungry, I walk to our house and drink a glass of milk made with powdered milk and water, find some bread and stale cheese to eat. Moses knocks at the back door and is holding okra and peas from the garden. The trader woman comes carrying a pan of fresh pineapples to sell. We will have food.

This evening we are eating supper with Alice and Bill. We eat at a table outside after sunset, when the air is cooler. A memory-making time. Later, Alice and I go to night market together.

As we leave, I turn and look for a long time at the market people standing or sitting by their wares where small oil lamps flicker. Dark as they are, they are almost invisible. The scene is like an unforgettable painting.

Wednesday, May 10th

In the night a gentle rain begins falling, unlike any I have heard since being here. I lie listening to the splashing of water on the teak leaves like water from a hose sprinkler turning back and forth. Leaning close to the open window by the bed, I can smell that rich earth odor I remember as a child when I visited on my grandparents' farm in Kentucky. Now I am so stimulated by the rain and earthy smells I get up and sit in the rocking chair by the window in the living/dining room. As I rock in the darkness, the words "all is well" keep coming to me over and over, and I am comforted. Centuries ago, Saint Julian of Norwich uttered these words as she lay dying after years of suffering.

Price is awake and comes to sit by me. We watch the dark break into light of day. Here the dismal gray light comes on speedily. Inky darkness, then a sudden grayish light, turning lighter. A different dawn, almost eerie, but a good thinking time.

After breakfast, Price and I go to chapel service at the seminary. Carl speaks in appreciation of our work with the students and remarks on how well we fit in with the life and work going on here. I am pleased to know that he thinks that of us. He presents us with a farewell gift from the seminary family. It is the handsome King Ebony mask—the one I admired in Benin City. He had written to Mildred Crabtree, while we stayed in Benin, to be watching to see what we liked. A very thoughtful man!

Gloria works here this afternoon. She says she is feeling better now that David and the children are well from chicken pox. She is so tiny, hardly five feet tall, yet is a bundle of energy.

In a way, I am sad to know she and her family will return to a small village in Ibo country, where she and David were born and grew up. Life will continue to be difficult for them there, surrounded by people with tribal beliefs. Gloria has a steady faith that God will provide and take care of them. I, too, must leave them in God's care.

Thursday, May 11th

Price is up reading in the living room. Electricity cuts off. I hear him bumping into furniture, trying to find a candle to light. I get the torch and wander in to help him. Roosters begin crowing in Mrs. Imasogie's chicken yard, and the funny-sounding bird that makes a noise like gargling in his throat is quiet. Dawn is on its way.

I look at the May 11 date on the calendar and pray silently "Lord, give me the strength to wait patiently for news about Sara." We are concerned, too, about our sons, each with his own problems but none as life-threatening as Sara's could be.

I like the verse in Colossians where Paul, writing to the church in Colossae, says: "May you be strengthened with all power, according to His glorious might, for all endurance and patience with joy." Strengthened with joy is a mighty big desire. Joy is so often spoken of by the New Testament writers. I think we miss the mark unless we have joy in our lives.

Joy has so much greater meaning for me than happiness. Joy is based to a great extent on gratitude, our gratefulness before God, I believe. Happiness is a pleasure or contentment associated with one's circumstances. Joy is essentially moral. It transcends our circumstances and is not dependent on them. The prescribed smiles we see on our TV screens are not what joy is all about.

Friday, May 12th

Awake at 3:00 A.M., cannot go to sleep again, get up, sit by the window until 5:00 A.M. I return to bed at 7:00 A.M. Price fixes toast and jelly and brings me breakfast in bed. A real treat.

Time drags. I am somewhere between departing here and arriving home. My mind dwells first in one place, then the other. In circles, in circles, that is how I move. My stomach churns and grumbles. I know our diet is a considerably poor one at present, and I know how "you are what you eat." All this makes me more understanding of how the disadvantaged in the world cannot function as well, mentally or emotionally, as the advantaged. It is all so sad.

Mr. Congdon is in Ogbomosho this afternoon. He comes to pick up our passports and registration cards. These must be stamped by an official in Oshogbo, indicating we are released to leave Nigeria. Hope there is no trouble or *wahalla* as the Yoruba say. We go to the Gaventas' house where Alice gives Price a haircut and does a good job of it.

Later Carl comes to take Price with him to see the *Sohun* of Ogbomosho. The *Sohun* is the chief of the village, like the mayor of a US city, but is called the King of Ogbomosho, in English. He lives with his four wives and numerous servants, and some advisors, in his new palace or large cement block house in the midst of mud houses, poverty and squalor. Carl told Price it is not polite for a resident visitor to fail to call on the King and pay his respects. Price is eager to go.

143

Saturday, May 13th

In the night, the sudden noise of a gusty rainstorm awakens us. White curtains at the windows fly out into the room like ghosts. This storm is equal to the state of my emotions. Never have I been more frustrated, not being able to get word about Sara.

Martha suggests we drive four hours this morning to Lanlate, a town where there is a satellite station. There we can make a long distance call to the United States. We almost decide on the long drive, then realize that if the baby has not been born, we will still have the anxiety of waiting to hear. There is no guarantee that anyone can get a message through to us here with the electrical situation so unreliable, affecting Telex communication. We can talk only three minutes at the satellite station for $16. I am sure I might cry, then Sara cry, and neither of us be better off for talking, if she should still be waiting for the baby. I decide to endure, endure. Carl says, "You will grow from this experience." A lesson in patience, I am sure. How difficult it is for the human spirit to wait for things to happen in God's own time!

We discover that one of the boxes Price has packed with books weighs over the limit of 22 pounds! He worked hours on getting the books wrapped correctly. He has to unwrap it and redo.

I go out for a walk alone before supper at Frances Jones. I turn down the road in front of our house, kicking at the dust now and then with the toes of my shoes. It does my frustration some good kicking the dust, like digging up dandelions out of our yard at home in early spring. In the distance, I see the fiery flame tree and pink and purple bougainvillaea covering a roadside fence. No one is here but me in the midst of silence and twilight. I listen to the silence and the way I listen is prayer. This time is church for me. Here I can be intimate with the Holy. Here there are no demands. God is. I walk back toward the house, lifted in spirit and my frustration calmed. I am enabled to wait more patiently. The world is so vast and mysterious and, strangely, one can contain all this only within one's own self.

Sunday, May 14th

Awoke to sun and a noticeable breeze through the windows. After breakfast, Alice comes to tell us that the Richardsons are driving to Lanlate today to make a telephone call by satellite to their son in the States. They were expecting him to arrive yesterday by plane in Lagos, but he did not come. They need to find out what happened. Alice says the Richardsons will make a call for us to Sara.

We know the Richardsons will not be returning until evening. Toward late afternoon I walk outside in the heat, foolishly looking for a car to turn in the driveway.

We walk to Frances Jones for a snack supper. Martha suggests we do some sky observing. She has studied astronomy and is knowledgeable about stars and constellations. Instead of stars, however, over the palm trees, we view a giant puffy white cloud shot through with streaks of purest blue, resembling low-lying islands. A sense of joy envelops me. Simone Weil has said, "Joy is the sweetness of contact with the love of God." And so it is this evening.

How many wonderful experiences of joy I have had in my life. Could I name them all? Music so often transports me into realms of joy. Once we sat in Christ Church chapel in Oxford and heard their choir sing Allegri's "Miserere." When a young boy's treble voice reached the high notes, I was soaring heavenward, filled with joy.

At 9:00 P.M., the Richardsons drive down our driveway, blowing the car horn all the way. I run to the door. Margaret yells out the window, "It's a boy, it's a boy! They are both OK!" She had gotten through by satellite phone to Sara! John David, our grandson, was born May 5th, on the day I sat with Benjamin under the baobab tree. We rejoice and rejoice over the news. Sara said they did send a message through the mission board by Telex to Ibadan, but evidently it was never received there. The reality of God's presence—my epiphany experience—will never leave me. I had come grudgingly across the world to an unknown land and truly experienced the love of God.

Monday, May 15th

At breakfast we talk about our new grandson. We are more alert physically and mentally this morning. Amazing how being under stress or strain can affect a person in so many unhealthy ways.

This morning Marjorie is having a farewell party for me at

Frances Jones, with eighteen of the student wives coming. Like everything Marjorie does, the games, songs, and refreshments are well-planned. At the end of the singing time, Anna comes and presents me with a tie-dye brown and yellow caftan to wear. To think that these women have pooled their meager resources to give this gift moves me greatly. A thank you is not enough. I tell them I am leaving money with Marjorie to help supply vitamins for student wives next year.

In the afternoon, Price and I drive down the highway to buy coffee and to air mail some large envelopes. We have been here for five months, which does not seem possible. We pass again the tin-roofed shacks that are stores, plastic buckets and plastic shoes piled outside, lorries and trucks on the streets. I regret to see plastic replacing the hand-woven baskets and leather shoes Nigerians formerly made and used. All the purple and pink plastic is cheap and gaudy looking.

An afternoon rainstorm drenches the garden. Hopefully the rain will help vegetables grow faster. Again at Frances Jones food is still scarce. We eat chicken casserole left over from Sunday and lima beans. Marjorie brings in bread for Price, who soaks the bread in liquid left from the beans to help satisfy his hunger.

Tuesday, May 16th

When I get up Price is at the dining table grading papers by candlelight. The large gray owl-like bird we saw in the tree last night, when walking home from Frances Jones, flutters by the window. Far off we hear a boo-hoo-hoo sound the bird must be making, which Thoreau believed to be "the dark and tearful side of music."

Mid-afternoon an elderly man, wearing a long, soiled white caftan and a blue Muslim fez on his head, knocks at the back door. He speaks English and says he has come from Kano with jewelry and thorn wood carvings to sell. I stand with him on the porch while he unties a spacious cloth bag. He claims the necklaces he shows me are amethyst and moonstones. If so, the stones are uncut, mostly resembling glass. Marjorie and Martha warned me not to believe what any of these door-to-door peddlers say about jewelry—that usually it is not the real thing. His bag is filled with necklaces of lavender stones, red crystal beads, and white beads he calls ivory.

When Price comes from his office, he reports that Carl says we will have to ride again to Ibadan tomorrow to have our visa extensions stamped officially, in order to leave the Nigerian airport. And I thought we were to go over that highway to Ibadan for the last time when we leave for Lagos and the airport.

Wednesday, May 17th

At 6:30 A.M. we leave with Carl in his car driving toward Ibadan. I sit in the back seat looking out the window at the landscapes of lush vegetation. We are passing emerald green palm trees and large-leafed vines wrapped around tree trunks. The vastness of this land should make a person feel lost. Instead, after five months here, I am experiencing a more close and personal kinship to it for some unexplainable reason. The stark and lonely beauty of the countryside does not overwhelm me now; instead it invites me to become a part of its mystery.

How often as parents we would like to resolve the pain our children suffer, realizing helplessly there is no way we can do this. Each person has to make his or her own way through life. Parents can only hope that how we have lived and what we have believed in will have an impact for good. I realize all this thinking is my way of praying this morning. I look left toward a pale blue sky filling with downy white clouds and intone the words, "all is well, all is well."

Sitting there, while Price and Carl talk together in the front seat, I recall Gloria's words yesterday when I told her Sara's baby had arrived. She was happy over the news, and we talked about the sweetness of newborn babies. I mentioned that Sara has two boys and was hoping for a girl baby.

Gloria stopped sweeping, held the broom, and looked me straight in the eyes. Her dark eyes flashing, she said, "God gives us the baby we need. God knows what we need." Words of wisdom, Gloria!

We arrive in the city driving through a street running with muddy water from rain last night, washing the land. Price and Carl go into a building where in ten minutes they get the visas stamped with our date of departure, May 21st. A long drive for such brief business, but the Nigerian government is very strict about regulations for departing this country.

Tonight we go to the Imasogies' for supper. The inside of their house is furnished in Western style. We sit at a long table set with white tablecloth, lovely crystal, and forks, knives, and spoons. We eat *moi moi*, jollof rice, chicken, fresh pineapple, and pound cake. I like Mrs. Imasogie. She is a good cook, and besides that, she laughs heartily and speaks English fluently. The evening passes quickly in the company of good conversationalists.

Thursday, May 18th

Last days before leaving. We are waking earlier and earlier as the time nears for departure. So many things to think about—the physical difficulty of getting through the crowd at the Lagos airport with our luggage and footlocker, the non-air-conditioned terminal, whether we have all necessary papers stamped, and the adjustment and culture shock for the first months in the US. We sit in the dark talking, waiting for electricity, somehow not wanting candlelight this morning. Price is concerned that I will get panicky if there is a pushing, shoving crowd in the airport. Something about being among bodies, pressing together and pushing, unglues me. Price reminds me that I must stay close to him and not wander away from the crowd.

We walk to the front of the administration building where students and faculty are gathering to have pictures made this morning. We each sit with our classes for individual pictures. The sun is bright, hot, the air humid, and it takes two hours to do all the picture taking. I find Patience and give her a blouse and scarf for a farewell gift. She thanks me and says she is not feeling well. She asks me to continue praying for her. I think she is weary from mothering seven boys.

Nat comes for the last time to wash our clothes. We give him a gift of money when he leaves. He has been faithful at this job.

After lunch, I go with Marjorie to the hospital for a baby-naming ceremony for Mrs. Bode's twin sons. Mrs. Bode has been helping Marjorie every morning at the Women's Building. Some days she would sit with her head on the desk, resting and sleeping. Marjorie says her husband is away in another country studying and sends no money to Mrs. Bode. After the naming ceremony, we load into Marjorie's car and drive Mrs. Bode several miles to a field where we see a low concrete block house in the distance.

Marjorie says there is no road to the house. We leave the car by the side of the road and walk single file under the searing sun to the house. Marjorie carries one baby son and I hold the other baby as we walk. Alice and Mrs. Bode follow behind, carrying gifts of baby clothes.

I am near tears as we approach the house and see the poverty. Bare floors, bare walls, a table and chairs in one room. Semi-naked children crowd around the doorway when we enter. We take the babies to a small room with one window, a bed, and a chair. We place the babies on the bed and leave Mrs. Bode sitting with them. Marjorie, Alice, and I are quiet returning to the car. We are sorrowful, not only for Mrs. Bode, but for thousands of suffering women in Nigeria. We are too depressed to talk.

Price and I are given a farewell party by the students this evening, a traditional custom here. Several students speak and one student honors us with a farewell address. Thomas, the writer of promise in my class, wrote the following speech for us, a beautiful one.

FAREWELL ADDRESS FOR DR. AND MRS. PRICE

May 18, 1978

With mixed feelings, we, the students of the Nigerian Baptist Theological Seminary, Ogbomosho Campus of Southern Seminary, Louisville, Kentucky, present this farewell address to you Dr. and Mrs. Price. As one writes such an address for such people of worth and value, there is a great temptation to resort to the use of superlatives but it is not etiquette, so I will not yield.

We could term it an uncommon manifestation of God's grace to have had this couple as part of our Seminary family for this laconic period of one semester. How we wish it could be extended. If we were Joshuas, we would stay the revolution of the earth to lengthen your stay. But that you must go is, for us, a matter of expediency to accept.

One would wonder why this constant sad note on our side. Perhaps a few observations will illustrate our contention. It is quite easy, Dr. Price, to suppose that you had been part of this school all of your teaching life. As you sit to prepare your lesson in your borrowed office or relax on a chair in the borrowed house, any one could call on you for help. Sometimes this borders on violation of privacy but each time, instead of reacting you would wear that million-dollar smile and throw in a welcome joke.

I can bet that many of your abundant supply of humor are not just laughable matter. Some of them are satires many are positive gentle rebuke and a few are pointers to heavenly truths. Blessed is that person who knows the difference.

When you came, standing head and shoulder above all else, a person remarked "if such a person should have knowledge, it would be a wonderful type." Without mincing words we can affirm that such remark has been justified. It is perhaps possible to see a theologian who is not a Christian but difficult to have a Christian who is not a theologian. It is still more rare to have both and more in one person. Frankly, we wish every student had tasted of your classes. Talking about you, one day with two professors one remarked "Every cell of that man's body is loaded with knowledge." And the other replied, "He chooses every word he uses." Thank you for imparting some of that knowledge to us.

We appreciate your soft-spoken, humble character. We hope to take your first commandment and apply it in every class. Namely "Enjoy the class." Your punctuality to each class, humorous comments at the beginning of each class, mini-sermons to drive each lesson home and your constant willingness to enlighten needy students after any class are blue prints of Christian love. We may not be able to express enough gratitude but accept us as we are. We assure you however that our faith has receive new impetus and you have affected us enough to Do Ethics.

And to you Mrs. L. Price, the school generally and the Writing Class in particular will ever remain indebted. It is great work having to combine teaching work with house-wifery in a foreign country—more so when the teaching is at night meant for rest. Such words as 'Beat,' 'Deadwood,' 'Lead,' 'Feature' meant only for the initiated, are among the rich legacy of intellect you have left us. The smile you have for everybody will continue to inhabit our memory long after you have left.

To both of you Dr. and Mrs. Price we give our heart-deep gratitude. Our spirits will go with you as you travel home. We submit you to the Lord for safekeeping guidance and ultimate reward. Goodbye.

Presented by Anyanhun, T.0.P.
on behalf of Student Body.

We are very appreciative of all the good things said about us but sobered, too, because we realize how much more is needed to help. We decide to leave money given us as an honorarium gift to be used in helping needy students.

Friday, May 19th

Before daylight a quiet rain descends. I have a headache, nausea, and diarrhea. I wonder if I picked up a germ at the hospital. Mrs. Bode lay her babies on a bloodstained operating room stretcher in order to change their diapers. Then Alice gave me one baby to hold who was wrapped in a blanket that had touched the stretcher. The heat and the odors yesterday were excessive.

Price comes to the house with the news that he has been asked to preach again Sunday, the day we depart Lagos, for the head of the Nigerian government, General Obasanjo, in his private chapel. We will leave Ogbomosho early Sunday morning with Solomon Abegunde, Obasanjo's chaplain, who will accompany us to the official headquarters. Mofeku will drive a second car, containing our luggage. He also will stay with us at the airport terminal in case there should be a hang-up or unexpected delay of days; then, he would be available to return us to Ogbomosho.

We go to a dinner in the students' cafeteria for the graduating class. Food is Nigerian fare of tough meat stew and pounded yam. I eat sparingly, still feeling queasy in my stomach. We stay late and speak with all the graduating seniors, who look happy but sad to be leaving. Over in a corner, someone turns on a radio's rhythmic music. I glance around and see David Ejenebo dancing, moving his lean body in perfect time to the music, a delighted smile on his face. There is music in his personality. How quickly and easily these people can dance. Here there should be a place and time for them to enjoy dancing. They have few places for fun and relaxation.

Saturday, May 20th

A cooler day, again like early June in South Carolina. I wash clothes we need for our trip, then begin the job of packing a large suitcase and a foot locker plus other small bags.

At 10:00 A.M., I stop work, dress and go to Okelerin Church to attend the seminary graduation exercises for seniors and for student wives who have completed two years of work at the Women's Building. Gloria marches proudly up the aisle when her name is called to receive her certificate. A commercial photographer is there taking a picture of each person as he or she steps down from the stage. For some reason the cameraman did not have his camera

151

ready when Gloria left the platform. After the graduation ceremony ends, I find her almost in tears. We go together to hunt the photographer, and I persuade him to take her picture, holding the certificate. We embrace and say good-bye. I think with great sadness that I will never see Gloria again, nor Patience, nor Benjamin, Thomas, Anna, David and so many more.

Thomas, Anna, and their three boys and his niece, a younger brother's child, come to see us in the afternoon. Thomas wears an American-type suit, shirt, and tie, and Anna looks glorious in colorful Nigerian skirt and blouse. All four children are shining clean and dressed in their best clothes. We make a family group picture of them standing outside our house in front of the tiger-striped bushes. We say fond farewells to each other.

Late in the day, Emmanuel Dahunsi and his wife, Deborah, visit us to say good-bye. They bring as gifts two handsome handmade leather foot stools, deflated ones to be stuffed after we get home with them. We are overwhelmed, so many times saying farewell today and now this endearing gesture of friendship.

We are to spend our last night at Frances Jones. From there, we will depart for Lagos early in the morning.

Tonight all the mission group will gather for dinner with us in the faculty lounge, a potluck affair. Another time of leave-taking. I have mixed emotions, wanting badly to leave and yet to stay, knowing how many needs are in this place, and believing we have been of at least some help.

Sunday, May 21st

In spite of excitement and a turmoil of emotions, I slept well at Frances Jones. We eat breakfast with Martha, Marjorie, and Lech on the familiar screened porch, where outside white lilies bloom and songbirds are tuning up. Sam has fixed a splendid fare of orange juice, bacon and eggs, toast and guava jelly to send us off in fine state.

We gather up our baggage. Matthew carries our foot locker outside, and we go to stand in the yard from where we have looked so many nights heavenward toward the sky spilling over with stars. A group gathers to say good-bye. Marjorie has decided to go with us to Switzerland, leaving from there for the US.

I look and see old Ba Ba coming into the yard to say his farewell.

"*Ek'aro*," he says as he grins and salutes me. "*Ek'aro*, my friend," I answer. This morning he is dressed in a long tan and orange caftan robe, not wearing his usual gardener's outfit of tattered shirt and shorts. For him to come dressed "fine, fine" is his way of showing honor to us, I am certain.

Price is to ride with the chaplain. Marjorie and I will go with Mofeku, with all the luggage divided between the two cars. I talk non-stop with Marjorie to keep my mind off the speeding highway traffic. In Ibadan, we stop for lunch with the William Benders, again saying our good-byes. From Ibadan we drive onto a new four-lane highway, only recently opened to the public. From there to Lagos, the drive goes smoothly with less danger from passing cars. We arrive in Lagos in a downpour of rain, which leaves the city hot and muggy and us feeling like being in a steam bath.

Marjorie and I leave Mofeku; he will meet us later at the airport. We ride with Price and the chaplain to Dodon Barracks where Head of State Obasanjo lives in military headquarters behind guarded walls and gates.

We are ushered into this compound through the opening of iron gates, guarded by armed soldiers. We are met at the door of a three-story rectangular stone and cement block building by an official who recognizes Abegunde. From an enormous entry hall we are led into a waiting room area, as large as a hotel lobby carpeted in red, wall to wall, with comfortable red plush chair and couches. While we sit and wait for the Head of State to appear, we are served orange juice out of cut crystal glasses. We sit for fifteen minutes or more, while men and women, some in Western dress, some in Nigerian dress of tunics or caftans, move in and out of the room, talking, laughing, and chatting in groups.

Suddenly from down a hallway, Obasanjo appears to greet us. He is a tall, heavy-set, muscular-built man with a commanding looking face. He wears a loose-flowing white caftan with brown designs. He shakes hands with each of us, then proceeds with Price and the chaplain toward his private chapel. Marjorie and I follow closely behind.

In a small room off the entrance hallway, we gather with ten other Nigerians and sit in auditorium-like folding chairs. A Nigerian plays the piano and a trio comes to sing hymns. Price reads scripture and has prayer. When he says, "Let us pray," Obasanjo and all the Nigerians in the room quickly get out of their seats, turn around, and kneel on the floor, facing their chairs. We do

153

the same thing. Each time there is prayer, we all kneel. Price preaches fifteen minutes. Outside the chapel door, Obasanjo shakes hands with each of us again, thanks Price, and we leave. The chaplain tells us Obasanjo is a devout Baptist.

Abegunde drives us through Lagos heading for the airport. People clog the sidewalks and the streets. In places, we move slowly, with the chaplain loudly honking the car horn to move people out of the way. Traffic moves as fast and furiously as in any American big city. Lagos is more modern than any place in Nigeria, with tall buildings looming on the skyline.

Mofeku is waiting for us in the airport lobby. We sit down and share sandwiches with him, which Martha has sent along. No place to eat in the airport for our kind of food. No air conditioning. We swelter while we eat. The lobby is a horror of heat, noise of people, and confusion. People appear not to know where to go once they are inside the terminal lounge. No signs are posted as to where to go or what to do. How much we take for granted when we travel. People must be completely bewildered who are entering here for their first time of air travel.

I sense that getting out of this airport may be another nightmare. I resolve to be calm. We say good-bye to Mofeku and the chaplain, then turn to go with our suitcases, bags, and our foot locker being trundled along by a Nigerian porter, with Marjorie following.

We pass without difficulty by a window where an official peruses our stamped visas. He looks at them, looks at us, does the same thing again, then in a loud voice says, "Go on." At another desk, a woman stops us to see the same visas, then sends us on. Marjorie has no trouble getting through.

Then we descend into a wide hallway jammed with people, as close as pickles in a jar, all of whom are talking, almost yelling, at the top of their voices. Some baggage is being placed on a counter, and men with heavy iron carriers loaded with what resembles enormous bales of cotton, are in the midst of this melee, pushing and shoving to get through the mob. I see that Price is embroiled in a shouting match with the man who was carrying our foot locker. This man has already loaded it on a carrier that will take it to our departure plane, Swiss Air. Now he wants Price to tip him in American money.

We have been told it is against the law in Nigeria for us to use American money, so Price insists on paying him in Nigerian money. The man is angry. They shout at each other. Sweat is

154

running down Price's face. One of the men pushing an iron carrier runs it close by my right leg. I am squeezed on either side by people pressing against me.

At last Price wins, and the man takes Nigerian money. Marjorie is ahead in the departure lounge waving to us. Price grabs my hand and pulls me through the crowd toward the departure doors. Inside is another world. No shoving, yelling mobs. People sit quietly, all is orderly. I breathe a sigh of gratitude that we are past all barriers.

Our flight is called and we pass another checkpoint before opening doors that leave us standing in the dark outside, waiting for the airport bus to take us to the plane.

In the distance, I see the sleek Swiss Air 747 bearing the insignia of the Swiss flag. We board the bus, alight, and head for the stairway going up into the belly of the plane. As I ascend the stairs toward the entrance door, I smell the fragrance of cleanliness. I could have kissed the stewardesses. Instead, I sit in my seat, buckle my seat belt, look out the window at lights that shine from the airport terminal and on beyond, seeing lights of the city. Like most journeying, one is at the beginning sad to leave the familiar things of home and sad at the end to leave a new place. What one discovers in between is what matters!

While the plane moves toward the runway, I am thinking of those friends we are leaving in this country, some of whom we will never see again. I think of the intensity with which we have lived for these months and of how daily we were needed. I think, most of all, on how God was real, so close to me in a mystical way I have never experienced before. I will always feel a deep and abiding gratitude for this time of making another leg on my inner journey. Now I affirm with T. S. Eliot, "Every moment is a fresh beginning . . . life is only keeping on."

Epilogue

Looking back now I remember those "winter" days in West Africa as clearly as if they happened only yesterday. Like the clicking of a slide projector, bright scenes flick easily onto the screen of my mind whenever my thoughts return to that time in my life.

For months after we left Ogbomosho, I kept in touch with several students and enquired through Marjorie and Martha about others. The mission group has changed since we were there. Many of those humble, kind, and giving people have retired or moved on to other work.

Nigeria itself still struggles in the throes of change—changes in the head of government, a slump in oil price which at its height brought wealth to the country and corruption among those in high places. It is, however, now possible to call by phone from Ogbomosho to Ibadan!

Yet the land, I am certain, remains stark and rawly-exposed under the blistering sun and silent, dark, and brooding under the light of the moon. And the people remain, in a sense, inscrutable, indomitable, and intent on survival whatever the circumstances, with a liveliness that is defiant.

Years ago I read of a French woman, Elizabeth Leseur, who made a journey to Africa with her husband in 1896, and kept a diary of her experiences. More than ninety years after her time there, I can identify with something she wrote. She believed and says in effect that she had an exquisite and unforgettable memory of the country. She thought that the life she and her husband lived there freed them from a city's stifling life and put them in touch with nature. But, most of all, she felt that Africa renewed and transformed her spirit.

Finally, and always, I remember that it was in Nigeria that I lived as Thomas Merton phrased it: "On a certain level of consciousness with the peace, the silence of aloneness, in which the Hearer listens."

DATE DUE